MANCHESTER PUBS

The Stories Behind the Doors

City Centre

Peter Topping & Andrew Simpson

TOPPER PUBLISHING

1

About the Authors

Peter Topping and Andrew Simpson have been working together for a number of years developing projects linked to the history of South Manchester. It is, as Peter said, a collaboration where he paints the pictures and Andrew tells the stories. Their work has appeared in venues across South Manchester, including an 80 metre mural, which was commissioned by a large building company and opened by Lord Bradley of Withington in 2012. Peter and Andrew also work independently.

Peter's work is much admired and he regularly exhibits his work, showcasing it on his website at www.paintingsfrompictures.co.uk

Andrew writes extensively on a range of historical subjects, contributing to various publications including Canadian ones and produces a popular history blog at www.chorltonhistory.blogspot.co.uk His books include a study of rural Chorlton in the 19th century, a book on Manchester in the Great War to be published in the February of 2017 and he has been commissioned to write the history of a well known children's charity.

Together Peter and Andrew have written Didsbury Through Time and are also working on Alexandra Park The Story which is due to be published in May 2017.

First published 2016.

Topper Publishing
39 Lambton Road, Chorlton-cum-Hardy,
Manchester, M21 0ZJ.
Tel: 0161 718 0193

ISBN 978 0 995705 50 0

British Library Cataloguing in Publication Data.
A catalogue record for this book is available from the British Library.

Typesetting and origination by Topper Publishing
Printed in Great Britain.

Contents

Acknowledgements

We would like to thank everyone that was involved in the research that went into the making of this book, especially Manchester Libraries, Information and Archives, Manchester City Council who gave us permission to use the black & white images throughout the book and the Digital Archives Association for supplying the old City maps.

A big thanks to Arthur Chappell for his old pub sign pictures and Deltrems on flickr for the 1990's images.

We would also like to thank the following people in no particular order whose knowledge and research into the pubs of Manchester was extremely valuable. Elaine Archer, Alan McCarthy, Paul Mitchell-Davidson.

Lindy Newns for many hours spent proofreading and editing.

And Peter would like to thank his Wife Linda for her understanding, and whose ominous task was to escort him and Andrew to many of the pubs they researched.

Last but not least a big thanks to CAMRA Central Manchester Branch for their help with the book sales and if you turn to the back of the book you will see an epilogue from them.

Introduction

Now pubs pretty much offer up all that you could want.

Of course most importantly they are a place to meet friends and family, have a drink and depending on the menu fill a few hours with some good food.

And of course they have always been one of the centres for a community, along with the church and later the post office.

But once they were also where the village or township might come together for an inquest or public meeting.

So when Mary Moore was "most brutally murdered" on her way back from the Manchester markets in 1838, the inquest into her death was held in the Red Lion in Withington, while the Horse and Jockey on Chorlton Green served the same purpose on several occasions, searching for answers into sudden deaths.

And in 1881 a representative of the Home Office travelled all the way up from London to the Lloyds Hotel in Chorlton-cum-Hardy to convene a public enquiry into the "Great Chorlton Burial Scandal".

The oldest Manchester pubs will go back a long time but many others date from the Beer Act of 1830, when in a move to combat gin drinking the Government made it easier for anyone to brew and sell their own beer.

The only requirement was that they would pay two guineas for a yearly license and after that they could make the stuff from their own home. The result across the country was an explosion in the number of beer shops.

In Manchester just ten years after the Beer Act there were 812 beer shops compared to 502 pubs which had risen to 920 in 1843 and a decade later stood at 1572.

In some of our streets in the mid-19th century there could be three or four such places often standing next to each other. Most were a short term response to a financial difficulty and lasted as long as the "crisis" but a few stayed the course and in time became established as pubs.

And that brings us to the 78 iconic Manchester pubs, some of which were well established before Wellington won his victory at Waterloo while others were still in the planning stage when the City hosted the Commonwealth Games at the turn of the century.

All of which we think adds to the fun of the book, which is not just a guide but a history of those pubs and the areas they served.

It is more than anything the story of the people who lived in them, worked in them and drank in them.

The 78 have been grouped together so that they form short "pub walks" and each group is accompanied by a description of where they are situated allowing the interested tourist to put the pub in to its context and learn about what made Castlefield different from New Cross and why the Northern Quarter still has more than its share of period pubs.

All of which marks the book out as a bit different and this is continued by the inclusion of a "Peter painting" for each of the 78 pubs.

And some of these paintings have themselves passed into history as the pubs have been redecorated taking on a new landlord and even a bit of a makeover inside.

But what remains constant are their histories and the affection they command from their customers.

The Old Nag's Head is one of those 19th century city pubs which is fondly remembered by many. For some it is the coffin which was a feature of its back room while others still talk of how it hosted the likes of Judy Driscoll, Long John Baldry and

Rod Stewart, all of whom rehearsed in a room upstairs before going on to play at the Old Twisted Wheel.

No less loyal are those who frequent the Knott Bar on the corner of Castle Street and Deansgate. It may not be able to claim to have been serving beer as long as the Nags Head but it occupies an arch in the railway viaduct, which was built in 1849, and the space under the railway line has been home to a shed load of enterprises including in 1966 the Modern Tyre Repair Company which supplied India and Goodyear tyres as well as a special deal on retreads.

But pubs are under threat. In the last decade plenty have closed and in the course of writing the book some of the 78 have served their last pint, bade farewell to their last customer and closed their doors for good.

We wondered about including them but they remain a landmark and it is just possible that by the time you read this they will have reopened.

So as they say "we commend" this little volume of the 78 in the sure knowledge that you will find the stories interesting, the pubs delightful and the walks instructive, with that added piece of advice that you can visit them in any way you want.

You can start each walk in a different way or be very adventurous and pick and mix, taking in one from each walk .... it is all there for the sampling.

This is truly a book for all occasions, all histories and of course all beers.

NEW CROSS

Packed with people that history
has forgotten.

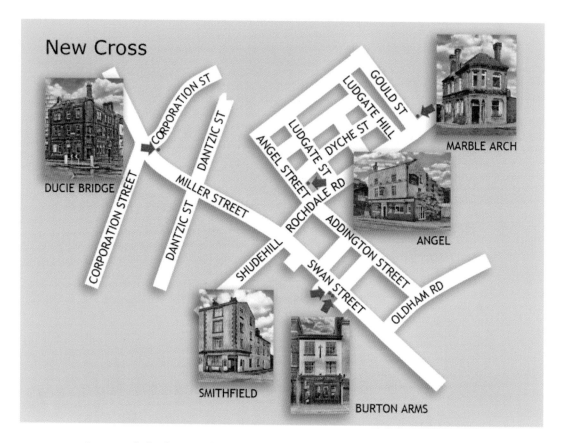

New Cross

DUCIE BRIDGE
CORPORATION STREET
CORPORATION ST
DANTZIC ST
DANTZIC ST
MILLER STREET
DANTZIC ST
SHUDEHILL
ANGEL STREET
LUDGATE ST
LUDGATE HILL
GOULD ST
DYCHE ST
ROCHDALE RD
ADDINGTON STREET
SWAN STREET
OLDHAM RD
MARBLE ARCH
ANGEL
SMITHFIELD
BURTON ARMS

An awful slum, the biggest wholesale market, a notorious street gang and five interesting pubs with a lot of history.

Once known at St Michael's Ward the area had grown in the space of less than 20 years and by 1794 the street pattern was pretty much as we know it.

It included Angel Meadow a slum so infamous that like Dante's hell all who entered might abandon all hope.

But there was also the Smithfield Market which sold "all that life could want" and off on Rochdale Road were the dangerous Scuttlers, a street gang who took their name from the road.

And for those wanting to compare their walk today with a stroll in the mid-19th century, Mr. Adshead's "Twenty-four Illustrated Maps of the Township of Manchester, Divided into Municipal Wards and Corrected to the 1st of May 1851" is a must.

It is according to one source "one of the cartographical gems of Manchester, aesthetically pleasing, fascinating in its detail, an object of beauty and utility freezing the great

'metropolis of manufactures' at the midpoint of the century".

Unlike the OS map for 1849, Mr. Adshead's map is in colour and is detailed enough to offer up the names of most of the pubs in our walks.

So here on Angel Street is the Weaver's Arms, which is now the Angel along with St Michael's Church and the names of the alderman and councillors who represented the ward.*

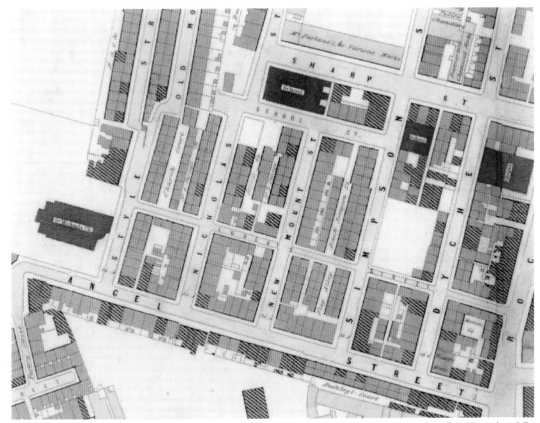

Angel Street and S Michael's Church 1851

*Terry Wyke, Introduction to Adshead's Illustrated Atlas of the Townships of Manchester, 1850-51, Digital Archives Association edition

Marble Arch Inn...

which was once the Wellington Inn Rochdale Road.

Now the Marble Arch is living proof that a pub with good beer can prosper.

Throw in a fine building which was awarded Grade II listing

Marble Arch Inn (Wellington Vaults) 1958

in 1988 along with some serious history and it pretty much has got the lot.

It was until recently called the Wellington Inn and, as the Wellington Inn back in 1850, its landlord Mr. James Jones could look out on a Rochdale Road dominated by textile mills, timber yards and a mix of terraced houses and dark courts, all of which would have been good news for this landlord with its promise of a fair number of thirsty customers.

Just next door was Jane Cockrane, who was a widow and who gave her occupation as a baker.

She shared her house with four others and, running down the road in the next seven properties, were another 39 people, most of whom were adults whom I suspect knew the inside of the Wellington all too well.

Of these, some inhabited the cellars of the houses, which, on a cold and wet evening, could not match the attractions of Mr.

Jones's emporium.

Just at the back of the Wellington was the Corporation's Gas Works, which, while it may produced some pungent smells, would also have offered up a heap of tired and thirsty workers, of which a fair few would have come straight from the coke ovens and coal yards.

In 1888, the old pub was replaced by the present one, which in 1911 was home to Mr. and Mrs. Ward. They were assisted by the 24 year old Thomas Gunning from County Sligo with help from the oldest of their five children, who all squeezed into its four rooms. And by one of those nice twists of history when the pub was having its makeover, there

behind the 1970s plaster board, were the original lime green wall tiles, which will have been familiar to the Ward family and

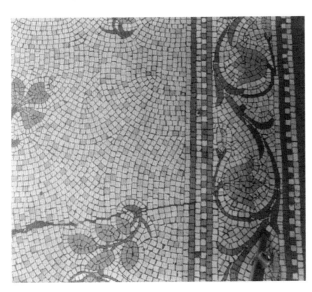

to countless customers from the gas workers and textile operatives to John and Ada Eccles who lived next door and sold apples, pears, carrots and potatoes and may well have sent their Helena in for a jug of beer to go with the Sunday roast.

The Angel...

or Mr. Bianchi's superior Weavers Arms, Angel Street.

I wonder what Mr. John Bianchi, who ran the Weavers Arms on Angel Street in 1849, would have made of his pub today.

Like quite a few of our pubs, it has changed its name and undergone more than a few makeovers in the last couple of centuries.

Perhaps the biggest change Mr. Bianchi would have noticed is the total absence of the lodging houses which ran down Angel Street leading off to that most notorious of slums which was Angel Meadow.

The street was narrow and many of those lodging houses were packed with people history has forgotten, if it ever took notice of them in the first place.

At number 44 in 1901 there were thirty two of them, all male, ranging from William Paxton aged 22 from Wigan, who described himself as a street hawker, to Thomas Reed from

Angel Street 1897

Ireland who, at 74, was still working as a labourer.

All of them earned their living from manual work or the slightly more precarious occupation of selling on the streets.

Most were single, although a few were widowers, and while the largest single group had been born here, there were those from the rest of Lancashire, as well as Ireland, Scotland and some even came from London.

And that brings me back to Mr. Bianchi, who just a few years before he started pulling pints at the Weaver's Arms, was living with his family on Tib Street. He had been born in 1788 and when asked his place of birth had said "foreign parts", which it turns out was Italy.

By 1847, he was the tenant landlord at the Weaver's Arms and, judging by the Rate Books, was not master of a palace, although he was paying considerably more in both rents and rates than his neighbours. Sadly, he died in 1849 and the family settled in a shared house on Fleet Street which was just

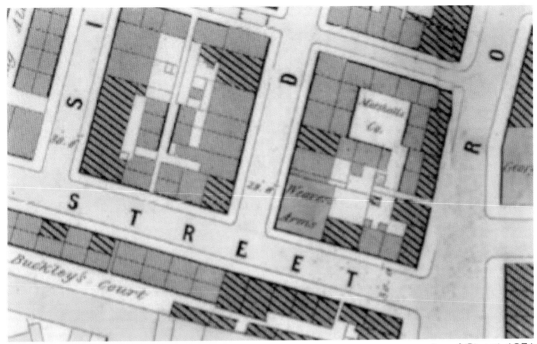

Angel Street 1851

off Deansgate, and along the way they anglicised their name.

The Weaver's Arms remained in business

until 2005 when it closed before reopening as a gastro pub and I suspect its future is fair, given that, with the coming of residential properties, the area is once again becoming repopulated.

I wonder what Mr. Bianchi would have made of that.

Lodging House, no 44 Angel Street 1897

Ducie Bridge...

has now joined the list of ghost pubs which have called time.
The Ducie Arms does rather dominate the corner of
Corporation Street and Miller Street, or rather it used to.
Today it faces the tall CIS tower while, behind it, is the new

Ducie Bridge 1969

Co-op building, which is "more glass than wall".

Even a century ago, it was dwarfed by the huge CWS stone and brick classical edifice on the other corner of the street and now by more and more blocks of flats, but these may well offer the pub a whole new set of customers as the trend to inner city living shows no sign of slowing down.

Not that I suspect the last landlord would have welcomed the customers, who John Ashton, the man behind the bar, had entertained back in 1870. They were according to the Manchester Guardian "thieves who were in

Ducie Bridge 1958

the habit of assembling in the pub".*

Giving evidence at the City Police Courts, Police Sergeant Potts said on one occasion he had seen "four convicted thieves, namely John Silk, John Harrison, Ellen Tucker and Margaret Tracey, besides 12 reputed thieves and a 'ticket-to-leave-man,' as well as men at the door of the house who, seeing him, ran in quickly and then others came running out".**

In his defence, Mr. Ashton claimed that, given that the area was in a low locality, "if I do not serve them, I may as well close

Ducie Bridge 1971

the house for very few come into the house except thieves".

And that pretty much sealed his fate. Mr. Ashton was fined £10, ordered to give security of another £20 to keep the peace for another 12 months and lost his license.

*Manchester Guardian March 30, 1870.
**Ticket of leave, issued to a criminal who had shown good conduct and was awarded certain freedoms including permission to get a job. Tickets of leave recorded details of employment and addresses.

Smithfield Market Tavern...
whatever happened to Mr Lythgoe?

Swan Street is one of those short but busy thorough fares that you can traverse in minutes and probably miss its three pubs, of which the Smithfield Market Tavern is the most interesting.

It stands on the corner of Swan Street and the even narrower Coop Street and back in the mid-1840s through into 1854, it was the home and business of Peter Lythgoe.

And I rather think he had made a sound choice to sell his beer from this spot, given that, directly opposite, was the Smithfield Market, which was opened in 1822 "for the sale of fruit, vegetables, eggs, cheese, dried fish.... with such a large trade being carried on that it would be difficult to point to anything in the three Kingdoms of nature, - animal,

Smithfield Vaults 1971

vegetable or mineral - that cannot be procured here [including] china, earthenware, tin and iron vessels of every description, glass, also clothes readymade, and calico fents, and boots and shoes".*

Added to which there was a warren of streets filled with

terraced housing and small courts packed with people and a set of timber yards, silk and cotton mills and smaller workshops.

Had we stood with Mr. Lythgoe and looked down Swan Street, we could have counted a

total of fifty-five properties and another eleven on Coop Street, all of which would have offered up a host of customers.

Smithfield vaults 1970

That said, there was a fair amount of competition. Next door but one down Swan Street was the John O'Groats House and a little further down was the George and Dragon, while less than a minute's walk away there were another seven, and there would have been lots of little beer shops operated from the family home and lasting in some cases for just a year or less.

So when you stand inside the Smithfield Market Tavern, give a thought to Mr. Lythgoe, who is recorded in the Rate Books as paying an annual rate of £125, which was well above what his neighbours were paying.

And you might also ponder on what happened to him, because, despite his appearance nine times from 1845 to 1854, in the rate records, there is little else save a tantalizing reference in 1841 to a Peter Lythgoe living with his family in Chorlton on Medlock and describing his trade as "brewery".

*Duffield H, The Strangers Guide to Manchester, 1850

Burton Arms...

once the John O'Groats House, Swan Street.

Just one door down from the Smithfield Market Tavern is the Burton Arms which is one of the few pubs where you can walk in through one door on one street and walk out through the door opposite onto another street.

And that was just as it was back in 1852 when Mr. Robert Halliwell was in charge. He no doubt kept an eye on both his Swan Street entrance and the Foundry Lane one.

But while he may have been familiar with the problem, the name

Burton Arms 1970

the Burton Arms would have been a surprise. He was the proud landlord of the John O'Groats, which by 1863 was the Grapes and sometime after 1886 became the Burton Arms.

If like me you enjoy being silly, you will have your pint on the Swan Street side perhaps acknowledging its many name changes and then make you way out by the other door.

Of course the more adventurous will wander back up Swan Street down Coop Street, marvelling at how narrow the road is before talking a left on to Forge Lane onto what is an even narrower thoroughfare.

And perhaps with a warning from Mr. Halliwell ringing in your ears, you could imagine the short walk up Forge Lane past buildings which were already old when Wellington defeated Napoleon at Waterloo and on to Tib Street and then to the junction with Great Ancoats Street, which was once a popular spot for public meetings and more than a few riots.

All of which might be a sensible plan in the event of our old friend Eric walking in through the door.

His favourite topic of conversation on the days we ran into him were the different colour schemes of the exterior of the pub. "Now", as he said for the third time between sips of his pint, "I have seen the outside go from a browny colour to a greyish one and then to a reddish one, and that is just within a couple of years". Pub conversations don't get much duller.

But to say any more is to stray into our next walk, when we plunge west across Ancoats.

Burton Arms Foundry lane entry 1993

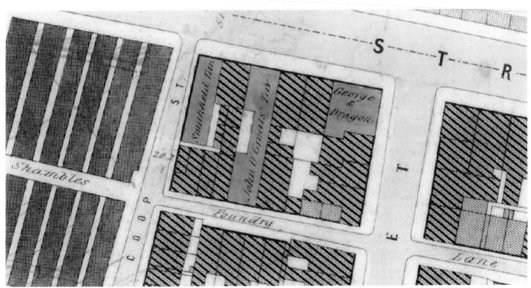

The three pubs on Swan Street 1851

GREAT ANCOATS ST
In the heart of The Northern Quarter.

Great Ancoats St

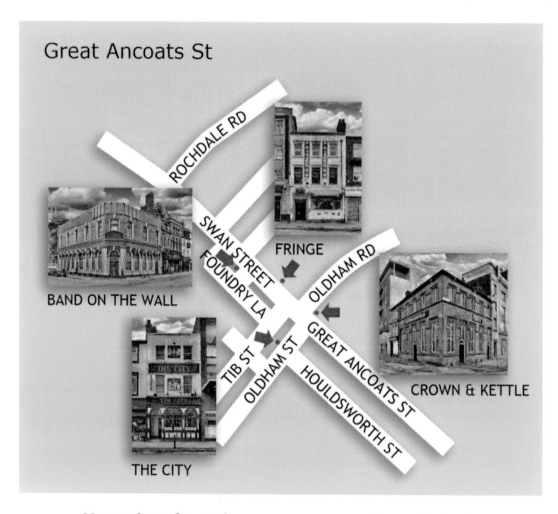

ROCHDALE RD

SWAN STREET

FOUNDRY LA

FRINGE

OLDHAM RD

BAND ON THE WALL

TIB ST

OLDHAM ST

GREAT ANCOATS ST

HOULDSWORTH ST

CROWN & KETTLE

THE CITY

Memories of pet shops, a new name for a historic area echoed by old pubs with changing names and, of course, that big, black glass building.

You can't miss the old Daily Express building on Great Ancoats Street where once the printing presses rolled, but it is really only a starting point, for the journey will take us around the edges and into the heart of what is now the Northern Quarter.

Two decades earlier, Mr. Adshead had recorded nineteen pubs along our route from Swan Street into Tib Street and onto Oldham Street and, of these, I think my favourite might have been the Paganini which stood on Great Ancoats Street between Port Street to Dean Street.

Part of my fascination for the place is that it was the pub with two names. Now that is not unusual. Maps from the mid-

19th century do show some pubs with two different names, but what makes the Paganini's story just that bit more interesting is that, for most of its existence, it was the Astley Arms and only appears on maps as the Paganini and then only for a short time.

As the Astley Arms it was certainly serving up beer and happiness by that name in 1822 when Thomas Evans was the landlord. And like the dual name he intrigues me because he had a full set of crockery made marked the "Astley Arms" and "Thomas Evans". The cups and plates were found during an archaeological dig of the site in late 2016 and the finds also included a stoneware bottle from J. Moorhouse & Co., Hulme, a glass bottle with the logo of a workman's arm and another bottle still containing brandy.

And that leads me to the George and Dragon, which is a sort of ghost pub, in that, while it is still there, it is now The Band on the Wall.

Daily Express Building 1939

Band on the Wall...

once and for a long time better known as the George & Dragon.

This is a pub I have fond memories of but, by the time I washed up there in the late 70s, it had become the Band on the Wall which had pretty much been its unofficial name for decades having become popular in the 1930s and 40s as a place to hear jazz bands and Italian performers.

In its time, the place has seen performers as varied as Art Blakey, Bill Bruford, John Cooper Clarke and the Fall along with many local musicians.

I can't remember whom I heard on the many nights I ended up there. It was just enough to get that heady mix of live music, beer and an informal atmosphere which was all about just having fun.

The Band on the Wall (George & Dragon) 1959

I rather think this would have appealed to the McKenna family, who had acquired the old George and Dragon in 1854 and expanded the premises into the adjoining properties on Swan Street and Oak Street.

Having opened in 1975 as Band on the Wall, it closed briefly in 2005 but reopened and continues that long tradition of music and good beer. My only regret was that I missed its

birthday party on August 4, 2000, when the Manchester composer Paul Mitchell-Davidson performed a special birthday piece in big band style.

Reflecting back, he remembers, "I have many happy memories of the Band. I was there from the very start and remember along with other Manchester musos helping Steve Morris move in.

"Of course in those days it still had the 24-hour license left over from the market trading days which I imagine later made the process of getting a late drinking license easier.

"All the local musicians used to meet at The Band before and after gigs.

"I played there countless times particularly during the 70's and 80's, so I was very honoured to be commissioned to write the 25th anniversary piece 'Shouting On Swan Street'.

"The title has obvious

musical connotations, but also refers to the less than social behaviour of some of us when leaving in the early hours!

Enjoying a studio session 1975

"Although essentially a jazz piece, it is also a sort of tone poem charting the many and various types of music that have been played there from the 19th century onwards. I like to think that the whole fabric of the building is suffused with music.

"As well as a 12 - piece band of top professional players, I also used some students from the Jazz workshop sessions at one point, and also a small gospel choir from the vocal workshop sessions.

"They sang a tribute to my friend Steve Morris 'A small man, with a big heart....'

"At the end of the continuous one - hour performance, there was a sort of stunned silence and then an amazing standing ovation which went on for about 10 minutes.

"I have to say that in all my 53 years in the music profession that must count as one of my proudest and happiest moments".

Now that sounds a good reason to visit Band on Wall.

The Fringe...

once the White Bear.

The Fringe is one of those narrow pubs that seems to have been squeezed into an impossibly small plot and makes you think it was an afterthought.

Not so, it has been on this spot for a very long time and, as the White Bear, it was serving its beer well before the mid-19th century.

Its small street frontage belies the fact that it stretches back and once backed on to Edge Court, which was one of those enclosed courts of houses where fresh air and sunlight fought to lighten the gloom.

From the back windows of the White Bear in 1911,

The Fringe (Old White Bear) 1970

you could have had a clear view of Edge Court's six very basic cottages and a glimpse of the Temperance Hotel whose address was no. 3 Oldham Road and boasted ten rooms.

On the evening of April 2, 1911, Mr. Reuben Caldwell of the Temperance Hotel had five paying guests, of which three were definitely passing through. These were Mr. and Mrs. Broad and Thomas Story. Mr. Broad was a dealer, and Mr. Story a "Gentleman". The remaining two may have been long term residents. Both were widowed and while Mr. George Stott aged 61 was retired, Mr. William Jones, aged 29, was a labourer.

Today, both the Hotel and Court have long gone and the space they occupied has become a car park, but the fine building with its rounded frontage which once stood beside the hotel is still there.

It was once the Manchester Joint Stock Bank, and part of it still operates as a private bank, and having looked at its entrance it just leaves that short walk back to the Fringe and the chance to sit in the small beer garden, from where, with a bit of imagination, you can call up Edge Court, and the Temperance Hotel.

All of which just leaves me to reflect on some of the features of the Fringe, which mark it out as just that bit different.

It starts with that long once fashionable chair in the window, the sort that you expect to be occupied by someone of elegance

striking a pose but which I suspect must have been very uncomfortable to sit on, let alone recline.

And then there is that period motorbike flanked by posters, which for me is eclipsed by what appears to be a giant green finger in the beer garden, but turns out to be an iron pillar much covered by ivy.

Crown & Kettle...

pretty much all things to lots of people.

The Crown and Kettle offers up more than just a historic pub. Just a little down Great Ancoats Street, stands the old Daily Express Building, which was completed in 1939. Its rounded corners and its mix of clear and coloured glass were best seen at night when all the lights were on and the printing presses were rolling.

And just behind it is the equally impressive Victoria Square Dwellings, which were completed in 1894 by the Corporation to house 825 people in 337 tenements. No less interesting is the low rise version close by, which was once called Sanitary Street but was renamed Anita Street after requests by its residents.

Crown & Kettle (Crown Hotel) 1959

All of which just leaves the area known as Little Italy which is off by George Leigh Street.

But that takes us too far away from the Crown and Kettle which can boast that a pub on the site was offering up beer from the 18th century. The present building is a delight to look at and has a beautifully restored ceiling in one part from the time it was a stipendiary court. This was done with help of

English Heritage after its long period of closure which lasted from 1989 to 2005.

And for those who want to impress their pub quiz team: The Crown and Kettle stands at the

junction of what was New Cross, which as everyone knows gave its name to this bit of Manchester.

But it was also, through the late 18th and into the early 19th century, a gathering point for public meetings and more than a few riots.

Following events in St Peter's Square, when a peaceful demonstration was attacked by the authorities, a gathering on the same evening was fired upon by the army resulting in at least one death.

On our last visit, we encountered a couple from Glasgow and their two friends from Yorkshire who were spending three days sampling the beer and the atmosphere of pubs from Oldham Street to Swan Street. They had a shed load of stories, some interesting recommendations of places to visit and the promise of each taking a copy of the book home with them.

Now they may have better memories of

Crown & Kettle 1986

what the place once looked like.

Sadly, I stopped going just before it closed for its very long period as one of our "lost" pubs.

I seem to remember the panelling from that airship, which was always a good talking point, especially when all other topics of conversation had dried up.

And the detail in the ceiling panels which interested Peter, seems to offer a glimpse of the pub's past glory.

But try as I could, my memory of the interior had faded, but to adapt that much used phrase about the 1960s, "if you could remember the inside, you couldn't have been there", or had chosen to drink soda water and lemon for the entire night.

48

The City 1972

The City...

a pub with more names than landlords.

The City is another of those tall narrow pubs which has a second entrance, which is handy if you fancy entering by

Oldham Street and leaving on Tib Street. But what really marks the place out as different, is that it once was two pubs, and went under a series of different names.

That said, by 1841 it was the Kings Arms and Coronation run by a Mr. Arthur Peters which became the Kings Arms Vaults by 1850, then dropped the word Vaults, eventually settling on the new name: The City.

All very confusing I grant you, which I suspect can only lead to another drink and another, by which time it will be play the game of choosing which entrance to leave by.

Of course the observant will have clocked the large painted panels high up at the front of the pub, which are well worth

careful study, and may even be worth a picture.

But just before you do that, there is that other test of a steady eye and a keen interest in pub detail, which is to check out the old plaster work around the ceiling at the back of the pub, which, according to staff, was restored on the advice of

English Heritage after a disastrous fire closed the pub for thirteen months back in 2005.

And that just leaves me to go looking for the book written by a previous landlord Rob Sutton called "A Tale of Two Cities", which contains stories and pictures of the place. Teresa behind the bar thought they had a copy but sadly she couldn't find it.

I just hope that when we publish the second edition of our book, his book will be included.

NORTHERN QUARTER

Narrow streets, the echoes of barrow boys and the lingering smell of fresh fish and ripe pears.

Northern Quarter

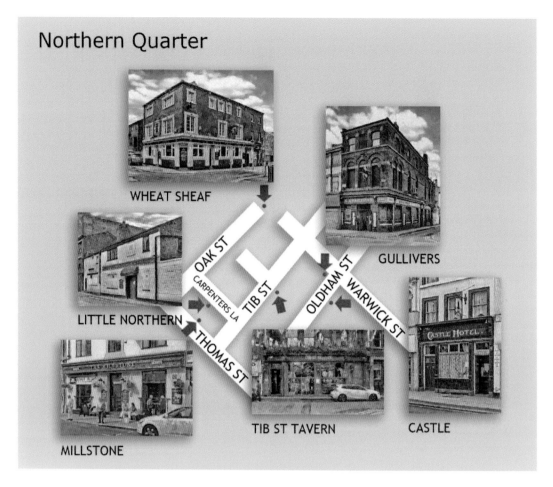

WHEAT SHEAF

GULLIVERS

LITTLE NORTHERN

OAK ST
CARPENTERS LA
TIB ST
OLDHAM ST
WARWICK ST
THOMAS ST

CASTLE HOTEL

MILLSTONE

TIB ST TAVERN

CASTLE

The barrow boys may have gone, and the wholesale markets are now just a page in a history book, but there is enough here to get a sense of what one of the older parts of Manchester would have been like, say a century and a half ago.

You can start on Thomas Street, which is narrow enough, take a turn up Tib Street, which gets narrower, and plunge off down Carpenters Lane, which just about takes a car and will admit no double parking.

Once, and that was not that long ago, the curious tourist might well have written off the area as a series of run down and mean streets fit only for the grand design of the town planner and developer, but all that has changed and now there are a lot of little quirky businesses, some interesting restaurants and cafes and of course a mix of historic and not so historic pubs and relatively new social housing.

And at the heart of it all is the Craft Market, which has been drawing people in since it opened in 1982, but for many, including me, it will always be the old retail fish market.

It was here that I saw for the first time an entire cod, which was a revelation, for here was no boil in the bag chunk of white fish or the battered alternative complete with chips, but the real thing – long, silvery and a giant.

The retail fish market had opened in 1873 and closed a century later, but, for those who want a bit of that history, two of the original fish mongers' booths are still there, complete with names and telephone numbers.

Today, the market offers an exciting mix of everything from porcelain and paintings to jewellery and sculptures. It is an ever changing place which makes it an exciting venue to visit, and, when you have visited all the studios, there is a cafe to relax in and plan the route around the pubs.

Of course you could take a picture of those fish mongers booths.

The rest have gone, but if you want a sense of those narrow streets outside the market, the Wheat Sheaf pub is a good starting point.

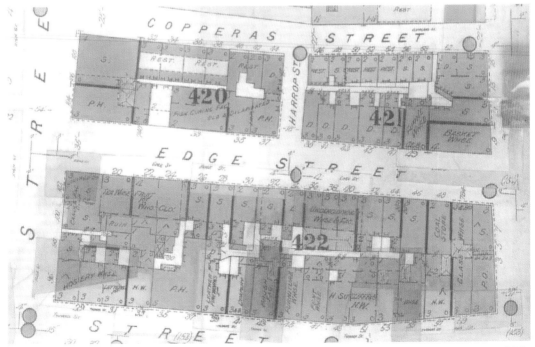

Copperas St, Northern Quarter 1880s

Wheat Sheaf Hotel...
tiled floor and ornate clock.

The Wheat Sheaf stands on Oak Street where the road takes a right angle and ends abruptly with a short but equally narrow pedestrian path, which was once Whittle Street.

The pub has a long history, although back when Mr. Adshead compiled his fine map of the city centre in 1850, it was the Fleece Tavern but occupied the same location and, like the now gone Queens Stores Vaults at the other end of Whittle Street, would have benefited from the thirsty workers leaving Smithfield Market.

The Wheatsheaf 1970

This may have been why, in 1916, it made an application to increase its drinking facilities, which, sadly, was turned down at the annual general licensing session in the Minshull Courts by the Justices.

And while it has nothing to do with the Wheat Sheaf, it is worth noting that the justices also acknowledged that it had become very difficult to get managers to run Manchester pubs, "owing to the large number of experienced

men who had enlisted or been attested".*

That said, Tommy and Jimmy who run the place today were very much the part of landlord and assistant and were happy to offer stories of the pub's ghost who Peter attempted to

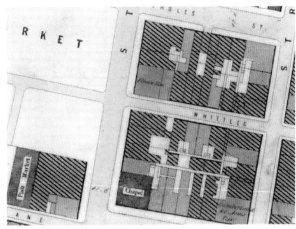

Wheat Sheaf (Fleece Inn) 1851

replicate with the assistance of Jimmy. The stories ranged from the ghostly appearance behind a glass panel to the stranger with the walking stick whom nobody saw come or leave and yet who made his presence felt.

I have no idea what the ghostly stranger made of the tiled floor or the ornate clock and surround above the bar, but I like the idea that they provide a continuity with the pub's past.

If you are minded for an alternative piece of history, just a minute's walk back along Oak Street to what is now Brightwell Walk, there stood a Chapel offering a different form of comfort.

*Manchester Licenses, March 3rd 1916, Manchester Guardian

Gullivers...

another of those pubs that have had lots of names.

It was once the Kings Arms and Coronation in 1850 when it occupied only part of its present site, changed its name to the Queens Stores Vaults a little later and, by 1911, had extended the length of Whittle Street from Oldham Street to Tib Street and, under the powerful eye of Mrs. Mary Alice Barker, was known as the Albert Hotel.

It has a period tiled floor, and a wooden panelled staircase leading to a large stage area all of which, as estate agents' literature says is a, "must see".

And I have to say that I do think its modern appearance is much better than it looked earlier last century. That standard signage we all took for granted (seen here in the black and white picture) was

Gullivers (The Albert) 1970

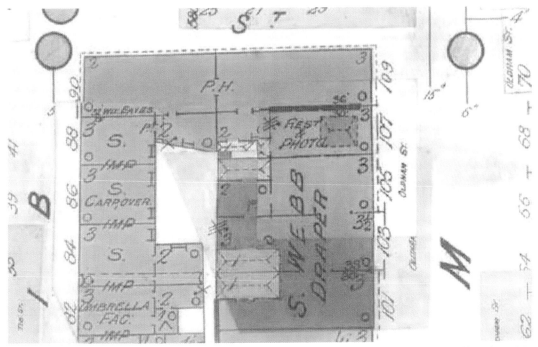

Gullivers (The Albert) 1880s

replicated in pubs across the city and beyond.

At the time, I suppose it looked modern, smart with the

promise of something new, but, as so often happened, the interior had not moved on from sometime just after the last war.

Of course, for some the interior is eclipsed by the exterior with impressive ceramic tiles of green and cream, while for others, it will be the knowledge that the place is owned by the former Coronation Street actor Rupert Hill who also owns the Castle and two others.

64

Castle Hotel...

back on Oldham Street.

Now, you don't have to rifle through the history books to spot that the Castle has a past, it just looks the part. The stories have it that it dates back to the 1780s; there was a building on the site by 1793 and it has had a variety of names including the Crown and Sceptre, the Crown & Anchor and the Clock Face, only becoming the Castle in 1936.

When our old friend Mr. Adshead wandered down Oldham Street in 1850 in the process of compiling his map, the place was called the

Castle Hotel 1970

Crown and Anchor Vaults run by James Preston.

And the place continues to reveal lost and forgotten secrets, so when the backroom was extended into the old lavatories to form a concert area, a very impressive fan light was discovered above

a false ceiling and, for those who venture upstairs, there is a fine room with an original fireplace which is reached by a narrow passageway with an ornate plaster ceiling.

Lastly, there is the beer garden which leads on to a back alley and offers up a mystery. The alley is Back Spear Street and it seems to have moved. On the 1849 and 51 maps, it is directly opposite Faraday Street and contained seventeen

properties along its length, which ran off Spear Street and then took a right to run parallel with its name sake, but, later in the century, it is shown behind the Castle, which I suspect is not a mystery to try to solve after a few pints!

Instead, there is always the disappearing business game, which starts when Oldham Street was a thriving place during the 1960s and is all about spotting the things that have changed.

By the end of that decade, C & A had moved off into the Arndale, prompting Marion Bowan of the Guardian to reflect that the, "metropolitan glamour of the Arndale Centre had left Oldham Street a bit down at heel". Very different from when the serious shopper could leave C & A's and wander up past the British Home Stores, dipping into a variety of shoe shops and furniture shops, put a bet on at the bookmaker, and choose from several pubs and a clutch of Yates's Wine Lodges.*

All of which is an introduction to a silly game which involves the 1969 street directory, which lists all the businesses on both sides of Oldham Street from Piccadilly up to Great Ancoats Street and the challenge of checking out what has survived and what has gone.

And if you only take the stretch from the Castle at 66 Oldham Street to Gullivers at 109, the result might prove the basis for a discussion on retail history, 1969-2016 and could prompt your companion to forgo buying their round in order to devise the board game.

*The high street that dropped out, Bowman Marion, The Guardian, December 12 1980

Tib St Tavern...

a Lambretta parked in the window.

If you are of a certain age, then Tib Street will always mean pets. Whether it was a cat, a parrot, or something that you thought was going to be even more exotic but turned out to be a goldfish.

I suppose it all means you don't always get what you expect and that is a roundabout way of

introducing the Tib Street Tavern which does not have the history of our other four but does look the part, which includes that

Tib Street Tavern 1959

Lambretta scooter in the window.

On a rainy day when the conversation with your friends or partner is going slow, the scooter may well spark an old story, although nothing compared to the one which I encountered on the streets of Naples, involving a grandfather, daughter with a baby and two boxes of tomatoes.

But back to the pub.

A full century and a bit ago, the site was occupied by A & B

Wholesale Upholstery with not a drop of alcohol to be seen. Go back another half century to 1850, and, while number 74 was home to Edward Cavanagh who was a painter by trade, just up at no. 66, Mr. James Pimlott was serving up beer from his front room and on either side at 56 and 78, Solomon Ashton and Jane Baron were operating "eating houses".

There are plenty of restaurants along this stretch of Tib Street to rival those of the past, so just maybe there is a bit of historical consistency, even if its selection of food is a tad different from what was on offer at Ms Baron's establishment..

But for many it will be the pet shops that define the street. My friend Rose remembers the pet presents bought for her as a child, but most memorable for her was the moment her mother decided to combine enterprise and two rabbits that has stayed with her.

It was, and I suppose remains, a simple plan which consisted of breeding rabbits. After all what could be a better money spinner? There would be the meat and the fur and, given the reputation of rabbits, it all seemed a plan.

It would only be a variation of keeping a family pig, which in rural areas in the 19th century, had been a real way of making some spare money while providing a supply of food for the family.

Rose, along with her sister and father, were unsure whether they would ever be able to part with the animals, and even then, Rose had severe misgivings about what was ethical and said she would have nothing to do with the exploitation of animals.

Tib Street from Dorsey street 1959

As it was, it proved a failure, the rabbits didn't like each other, the expected bevy of baby rabbits never appeared and her mother returned the two to Tib Street.

The Millstone...

offering up beer for a couple of centuries.

    By the mid - 1790s, Thomas Street was busy and open for business, and just sixty year later, it offered the discerning resident a choice between the Millstone, then named Mill Stone, and the White Lion at number 15, the Bay Horse at number 35 and the Wagon & Horses across the road at number 16, all of which meant that the streets mix of shop keepers and tradesmen might well swop tales of the fluctuating ups and

The Millstone 1970

downs of selling leather
goods and making
umbrellas and cabinets, to
the hardships of
hammering metal or
painting houses.

Whenever we have
visited the pub, it has
always been full, which

must be a pretty good indication that all is well in the Millstone.

It isn't a pub I ever went in and so it is a mystery to me, but I would love to know what the pub looked like in the past. The low ceilings give a clue and, only recently, the back room has been opened up as part of the pub, and I like the large fire place which dominates it. For others, however, it will be the windows that open out onto the street which will appeal.

On a warm sunny day, the table beside those windows is never empty and from the road

it acts as a magnet to passersby to call in for a drink. And that isn't the only thing which draws people in because Ged the landlord offers live music on many nights and performs himself.

The Millstone 1990

The Little Northern Hotel...

now part of The Millstone.

When Peter first floated the idea of a story, he was told to "ask the publican". I am also intrigued as to what Mrs. Edith Wright, who ran the Millstone a century ago, might have said.

The pub had fourteen rooms, which suggests an interesting set of enquires about how those rooms were used. Some, at least in 1911, were home to the four staff she employed.

And Ged Ford, who runs the place today, has a host of stories about both the hotel and the Millstone, along with tales of his other pubs, from the Black Lion in Salford to the bar in the 16th century Hough End Hall in Chorlton-cum-Hardy.

We went looking for a picture of the back of the hotel, but sadly no one ventured down there with a camera and so this one is the only image of the street or any of the buildings.

Carpenters Lane 1908

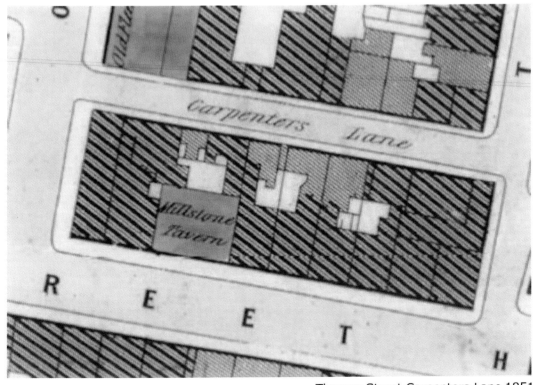

Thomas Street Carpenters Lane 1851

SHUDEHILL
Walking the edges of what was
once a warren of tiny streets.

Shudehill

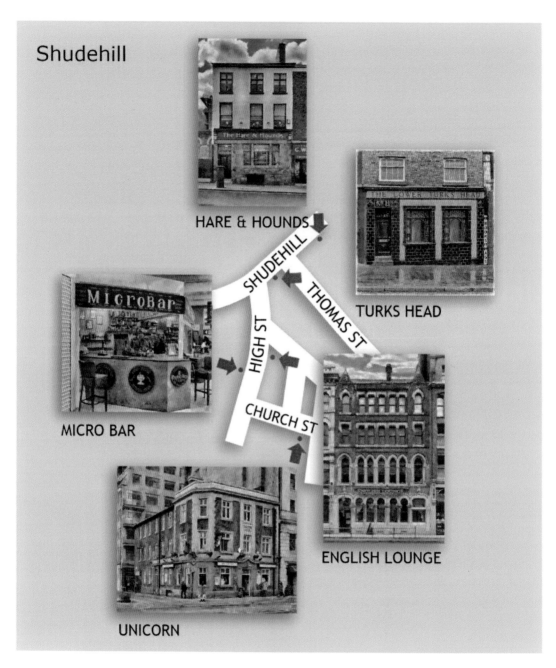

HARE & HOUNDS

TURKS HEAD

MICRO BAR

CHURCH ST

ENGLISH LOUNGE

UNICORN

Taking in the Hare and Hounds, the Lower Turks Head, the English Lounge, the Micro Bar and the Unicorn, or for those with the map... from Shudehill to Church Street via High Street.

Walking the edges of what was once a warren of tiny streets with fascinating stories and picking up on a tram stop and a bus station.

Now if you arm yourself with a map of Shudehill be careful to check the date, because, if it's any older than the late 1960s, you might get so lost and so confused that any one of these five pubs will be a necessary place to stop and get your bearings.

Once, and we are only talking a few decades ago, there would have been much to see on the stretch which ran south from Shudehill to Market Street and was bounded by New Brown Street to the east, High Street to the west, and was cut through by Cannon Street.

There were fifteen streets of various widths and lengths, one court and two squares and they offered up a mix of buildings and businesses.

Looking at the old maps, the recurring theme which crops up is the description "various" for the use of these properties. By far and away the biggest collection were the warehouses dealing with lots of different things, but there were also three printers, an umbrella works, some plumbers merchants and a mantle factory.

And of course pubs, which, along with a clutch of restaurants, will have done a good trade. In Palace Square, there was a Yates's Wine Lodge and close by the Mosley Arms run by Mrs. Ann Norman, which in turn was just six doors down from the grand sounding Gradwell's Restaurant at numbers 2-8 Shudehill.

Not that any are there now, because that whole swathe of this bit of busy Manchester is now under the Arndale Centre, all of which means that the best the curious traveller can do is wander the edges, starting at Shudehill and by degrees wandering down High Street and over to Church Street.

However, there is a sort of connection with that past and it comes in the form of the Shudehill Metro stop which is a reminder that trams are back in Manchester.

It took just over 40 years for them to return and they look nothing like the old tall and stately ones of the Manchester Corporation Tramways Department; they run on rails, are powered by electricity and are far nicer than the trolley bus which briefly succeeded them.

Of course, if you still prefer the bus, Shudehill also boasts a new bus station which most of us think is a distinct improvement on the Cannon Street one, which vanished with the building of the Arndale extension.

The Hare and Hounds ...

three small rooms, a shed full of interesting people and the story of the coach to Ashton-under-Lyne.

The Hare and Hounds is just opposite the metro stop and, with its tiled exterior and three small rooms, it looks the part.

We fell in on a Tuesday afternoon and each of the three rooms was full of customers, from the man who said no to the Beatles, to the lady who had taken the tram from Ashton-under-Lyne to spend the day with her friend from Ancoats, and I have to say that here there was that little bit of history popping up and tapping you on the shoulder because, had our lady from Ashton been

Hare & Hounds 1970

in the pub a century and bit ago, she could have waited outside the pub for the daily horse drawn coach service to Ashton operated by Mr. Silas Marlond and his partner Mr. John Andrews, or taken the rival service operated by Robert and Thomas Platt

and, if these didn't fit the bill, there were another four companies leaving from nearby pubs on Shudehill and Withy Grove.

I was all ready to go into the details of the journey to Ashton by horse drawn coach, but instead

I struck up a conversation with the man at the bar. Once he knew we were researching old pubs, he began talking about those beer pumps with a glass window which showed the beer and the mechanism moving from side to side, and went on to wax lyrical about using the outside urinal on cold winter nights. "It was", he said with a smile, "what made you appreciate the beer all the more".

And if you are of a certain age, you will also remember that outside lavatories came as standard in the homes of working people well into the 1950s, which in turn will remind many of the chamber pot. Now, at my grandparents' there were two

types, the porcelain one and the tin one.

Both had their good points, with the porcelain being heavier and therefore, when I was a child, easier to sit on, but somehow not as warm as the metal one.

And those outside lavatories extended into schools, and, however impressive and solid those old Victorian Boarding Schools were, they came with outside lavatories. Not that, in my school days, the onset of cold winters and frozen pipes did anything to effect the closure of schools as it does today.

Hare & Hounds 1990

Mr. Heatherington, the caretaker, performed his magic on the solid water supply with a carefully applied blow torch, done very gently and sparingly, which I suspect would also have been how those in the pub were treated.

Back then, looking out of the Hare and Hounds waiting for the pipes to unfreeze, the scene would have been very different. Instead of the metro stop, there was a slab of buildings which, in the late 19th century, were home to several warehouses specializing in everything from toys and brushes to rope and boots.

The Lower Turk's Head...

all tiles and history with an eye to the future.

It stands to reason that, if there is a Lower Turk's Head, there must have been an Upper Turk's Head, which of course there was. It stood on the opposite side of the road, five doors up from Hanover Street and post dated the Lower Turk's Head, having opened sometime in the 1820s, but it was gone by 1903.

Today, in its place is one of those serviceable early 20th century buildings which is shared by a small supermarket and a tattoo studio.

So - game set and match to the Lower Turk's Head. That said, it too 'went dark' for a while but has reopened and extended into next door.

I have to say it really looks the part with those glazed tiles and equally striking name and the initials of the Manchester Brewery picked out in contrasting colours on the exterior wall. Not that I would ever suggest that the interested tourist should ponder long outside the pub or for that matter on the stretch from The Lower Turk's Head down to The English Lounge on High

Lower Turks Head 1970

Street. The traffic is heavy, the views uninspiring and so the best thing to do is put on a pace for the English Lounge.

But before we leave, I must say I do like the way that the additional rooms which were added when the pub was

extended have kept much of the atmosphere of the original and the use of those old glass trade signs, which are in green picked out with gold lettering, along with the tiled floor, make the extension look special.

And on the day we visited, there was that mix of the earnest beer drinkers with a group of eight friends out for the day in the city. If shopping in the Arndale had ever been part of the plan, it had long ago been ditched for the pleasures of the pub.

English Lounge...

once a hotel with more than a bit of a past.

The journey from the Lower Turk's Head down to the English Lounge is less than scenic. First, you have the short walk across what was once known as Nicholas Croft and today is that busy open spot flanked by the Arndale car park on one side, some tired looking buildings on the other, and the very busy High Street with its frequent passing trams.

Survive all that and you will arrive

English Lounge (Wheatsheaf) 1970

at the English Lounge.

Now, my old friend Walter was forever complaining about the way that some pubs seemed to change their name with regularity, which both confused and annoyed him.

91

It wasn't so much that the new name bore no relation to the original, but more that it marked the passing of a bit of his youth and, on occasion, left him wondering where his old haunt had been, which is pretty much how I felt when I first walked into the English Lounge.

Like Walter, I had to think twice before I could place the pub which I remember as the Hogshead and many more will know as the Wheatsheaf, and, as the Wheatsheaf, it was offering up pints, food and good company by 1850. In 1885 it was advertised as the "Wheat Sheaf Commercial and Family Hotel, replete with every modern convenience".

Poster 1885

Back then, the hotel guest would not have been confronted with a view of the tiled exterior of the Arndale. Instead, there would have been a row of Victorian buildings housing a range of businesses from Fred Isherwood's boot and shoe company to Misses Frances and Alice Dickens, dealers in felt, and a clutch of tailors and blouse makers.

Sadly, none of the original interior has survived but, back in the 1990s, one employee came across "a lovely Victorian staircase which led to about eight to ten small bedrooms".*

*Michael Farrand.

Micro Bar...

bright new and different.

There will be those who are picky about what constitutes a pub and in particular one that does real beer. My friend Eric always maintains that you can only really call a place a pub if its walls still bear the traces of nicotine, there is at least one murky story about a past landlord and, for good measure, it has been under the threat of demolition by a developer.

None of which can be said of the Micro Bar, which sits happily in the Arndale Centre, offering a range of interesting beers and ciders to a mix of those who like the real thing and those escaping the third trek around the shops.

And after the third glass of their finest draught cider Eric wanted to know just what we had lost when the Arndale was built, and, quick as a flash armed with my map of 1851 we left the Micro, promising to return in half an hour and set off into the interior of the shopping Mall.

Micro Bar (Watts Bro) 1965

Of course it is impossible to recreate the tiny maze of back streets and passages which existed before the site was built, but with a bit of imagination and Mr. Adshead's detailed map we had a go.

Running directly east, almost parallel to the route that leads through the shopping centre, was Friday Street, which joined Watling Street and, by plunging north along this street, you passed a series of small entries including the one that gave access to Spring Alley.

But given Eric's interest in old pubs our destination would have to be the three which are roughly underneath Exchange Court in the Arndale. Of these my favourite must be the Higher Ship, followed by the Grove Inn, but the one I suspect Eric

would have preferred was the Mosley Arms on the corner of Watling Street and Shudehill.

That was partly because he remembered it and because of the iron railings which ran alongside most of the downstairs windows, which he maintained gave it class. These were ornate fiddly things finished off with an arrow design.

It was one of those old fashioned, no nonsense places with the bar just a few paces in from the main doors. Eric waxed lyrical about Cornbrook Ales which had supplied the beer and which had

High Street circa 1900

started up in the 18th century. The brewery was registered in 1885 and, after modest acquisitions of other breweries, was bought up by Charringtons in 1961 and finally closed in 1973, round about the time the Mosley Arms called it a day. Amidst all of Eric's reminiscences, I was just able to point out that, close by between Watling Street and Shudehill, was the old Hen and Poultry Market where the birds were displayed in cages.

That done, we retraced our steps to the Micro, which Eric liked, even if it lacked the iron railings with their fiddly bits and clearly had no nicotine stains.

The Unicorn...

hard by market stalls selling everything from fruit to second hand books and, of course, Afflecks Palace.

Now, there has been a pub called the Unicorn on the corner of Church Street and Joiner Street for a very long time. Back in 1841, a Mr. Ralph Hales was selling pints and dispensing conversation. He was still doing this a full twenty-one years later, by which time he had seen off two different owners and no doubt

seen a fair few changes in the area.

Sadly, we have no pictures of his pub. There is one taken in 1925, but this is not the one you see today. Back then, it boasted fourteen rooms over three floors and sported a number of Swiss style shutters to the upper windows, which, if I am honest, did little to enhance the look of the building.

It was a simple brick box with an entrance on Church Street which was accessed by a flight of steps.

The Unicorn 1971

The present pub almost follows the same basic layout with just a slight difference in the exterior design. Inside, it is as it always was, a pub full of locals who just enjoy meeting up and passing the time of day. They are a friendly bunch and, the last time I was there, I struck

up a conversation with one couple who argued over the relative merits of the different shops in Afflecks Palace, the future of the Northern Quarter and the part played by the

mythical Unicorn in the history of fantasy novels.

I wish we had got round to talking about that bit of sculpture just a bit further down Church Street where it joins Tib Street. It was an imaginative leap for someone to retain the entrance to the warehouse which stood on the spot and a bit more imaginative to add the ironwork above it, and it fits perfectly with the slightly quirky style of the area, from those wall paintings which are all over the Northern Quarter, to the use of ceramics for the street names and, above all, the interesting businesses, bars and restaurants.

I remember the wall before the addition of the ironwork, when it was less a bold statement and just a place full of tatty and peeling posters advertising gigs long gone and bars that had ceased to exist.

By contrast, the Unicorn has proved its staying power. In 1821, a Mr. Froggatt was behind the bar and still doing the business a decade and a bit later, and, given that there was a

building on the site by the late 18th century, the Unicorn may indeed be one of our oldest pubs.

Back then, that corner of Tib Street and Church Street had a well appointed set of gardens, which will be something to tell that couple next time I buy them a pint.

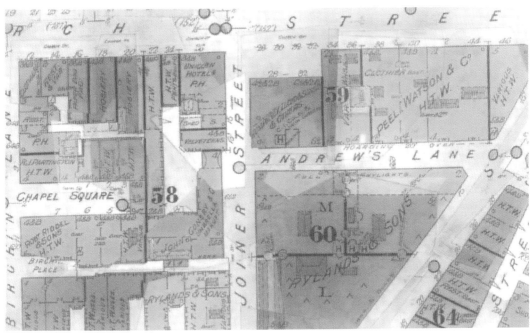

Church Street circa 1900

EXCHANGE SQUARE
An interesting fountain, nice furniture,
four historic pubs, the Cathedral and
a museum for the 21st century.

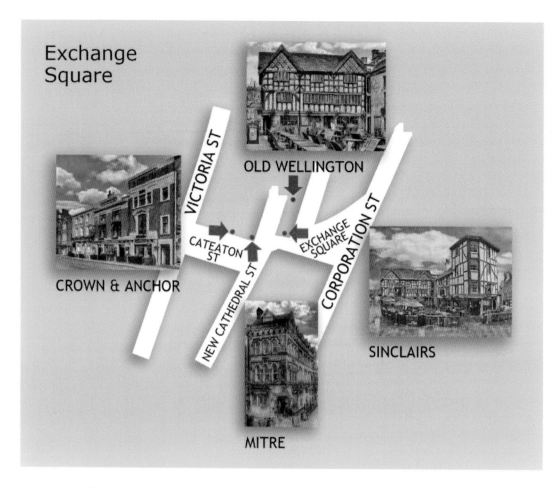

Exchange Square

OLD WELLINGTON

VICTORIA ST

CATEATON ST

NEW CATHEDRAL ST

EXCHANGE SQUARE

CORPORATION ST

CROWN & ANCHOR

SINCLAIRS

MITRE

The square is perfect testimony to that simple observation that, out of a pretty awful and destructive act, can come something to the collective good.

Before the IRA bomb in 1996, the stretch across from Corporation Street towards the Cathedral and along to Market Street was a pretty dismal spot.

At the beginning of the 20th century, the area was dominated by the Corn Exchange fronting Hanging Ditch and a series of buildings and small courts, alleys and narrow streets with magic names like Bulls Head Yard, Cock Pitt Hill and Blue Boar Court.

They had all the mystery of any twisty Medieval street and of course included the Old Shambles and that timber framed building dating from the late 16th century, but by the end of the 1960s, the area had been transformed by a series of buildings which, at best, were functional and pedestrian and, at worst, were just very ugly. Of these, Longridge House offered up a slab of a building with little grace or beauty.

It faced the more elegant Commercial Chambers built on a triangular plot of land surrounded by Corporation Street, Hanging Ditch and Cannon Street.

The one attempt at landscape improvement, consisting of a fountain near to the Commercial Chambers, attracted its fair share of windblown litter and just seemed to add to the general air of seediness.

But for those who really want to award the badge of bad design and urban poor thinking, that must go to those who managed to relocate that fine 16th century building with its 18th century counterpart to what was little more than a canyon flanked by the back of Marks and Spencer's and some equally innocuous mix of shops and offices.

On a cold wet day, there was nothing inviting about this open space and, even on one of those warm sunny days, the addition of a few big umbrellas and wooden benches did little to either lift the gloom or enhance those timbered gems.

The bomb gave Manchester the opportunity to sweep all that away and, for those wanting to arrive in style, nothing can be better than the tram down from St. Peter's Square or up from Victoria Railway Station.

Either way, the tram stops directly in front of Exchange Square and offers a fine view down to the National Football Museum, which was once Urbis and celebrated all that was exciting about urban life.

More importantly, it is just a short walk across the square to our four pubs, starting with Sinclairs and the Old Wellington, and on to the Mitre and the Crown and Anchor.

Exchange Square 2002

Sinclairs Oyster Bar and The Old Wellington Inn...

from a building that predates the American Declaration of Independence to another which was already eight years old when the first Elizabeth became Queen.

Now, if you are unlucky and Eric has finished early from his job in the Arndale, you might well get his famous hour long lecture on the history of the two buildings, only made possible by the pints you offer to buy him.

Sinclairs 1958

He isn't always accurate with his dates, nor should you believe his stories of ghosts or the night Bonnie Prince Charlie got thrown out of the Old Wellington, but suffice to say that Sinclairs was built sometime in the 1720s, and the Old Wellington weighs in at around 1550.

We will start with Sinclairs, and to put the story straight, unlike Eric, I shall quote the sources which begin with Mr. Frangopulo who drew on F. S. Stancliffe's John Shaw's 1738-1938. Writing in 1962, Mr. Frangopulo fondly wrote of Sinclairs Oyster Bar that it, "belongs to the

aristocracy of shops which can afford to neglect their
appearance, and the black–leaded kitchen range which

Shambles 1969

occupies one end of its principled room testifies to its refusal to be modernised".*

Sinclairs was open from the eighteenth century, "when St Anne's Square was still a cornfield. Fops and rakes as well as staid citizens, heard there the news of the 'South Sea Bubble', heard too, that 'Bonnie Prince Charlie' was marching on Manchester, and saw

Sinclairs 1962

the heads of the Jacobite supporters on the porticoes of the Exchange .... In those days, Sinclairs was John Shaw's 'Punch House' and the first and foremost club in Manchester, but later it was consecrated to the oyster, the lobster and the crab".**

The Old Wellington Inn

Eric is on firmer ground with the Old Wellington and accurate when he tells you that it was moved from one location to another but not that he fell asleep in the pub on the night of the move, only to wake up the following morning on the new site. On a good session, he will embellish the tale, but never ever tell his listeners that the buildings were carefully dismantled, and painstakingly re-erected over a period of time.

His account of the move may be a fib, but the truth never spoils the story nor takes away his concluding dramatic flourish

Wellington Inn 1897

as he points to the fine wooden panelling and makes an outrageous claim that William Wordsworth came up with the idea of "Daffodils" while sitting in front of them.

On a sunny Saturday, there will be lots of people sitting out in front of the pubs enjoying the views across to New Cathedral Street and over to Exchange Square, any one of whom may not have heard Eric's tales.

I doubt Eric ever bothered with either of the two history books and is also very light on the story of the Old Wellington. Bits of it may date back nearly 700 years, an assertion based on the discovery of one old oak beam found during restoration which carried the date 1328.

Now I am the first to admit that, back then, timbers of buildings were re-used, so maybe the jury is out on the exact date of the building, but I do know from a short account of the pub published by the Cornbrook Brewery in 1950 that the house had been occupied by the Byrom family, who carried out a drapery business in the property.

Around 1830, it became a pub and was known as The Vintners Arms run by a William Duffron, and like many of our pubs had its name changed and became Kenyons Vaults and then the Old Wellington in the 1850s.

*N.J. Frangopulu, editor, Rich Inheritance, 1962, & F. S. Stancliffe, John Shaw's 1738-1938
**ibid Frangopulo, 1969 edition page 198

The Old Wellington Inn 1958

Mitre Hotel 1958

The Mitre...

the building facing three ways.

The Mitre is what it says - a proper hotel with beds and all that follows for a good night's sleep in the heart of the city. This marks it out as different from many pubs which say they are hotels but are not. My Goad's Fire Insurance map, dated 1900, shows the hotel wrapped itself round other premises and ran from the corner of Cateaton Street along Cathedral Gates and faced on to Old Church

Yard. All of which meant that, if you got a room at the back, you had a fine view of the church yard and the Cathedral and were close to Hanging Ditch with its stone arch.

Added to which, you might be fascinated by the story of Hanging Ditch and after that good night's sleep, wander down to get a look at the stone arch and then on to the Cathedral.

Hanging Ditch is well worth a look and the more energetic might well then take the short trip over Victoria Bridge, past the location of a set of fountains which until recently was a

drab and uninviting car park, into Salford, and some interesting old pubs.

But they are not Manchester pubs, and outside the purview of the book which means you should retrace your steps to the Crown and Anchor which sits next to the Mitre. The highlight of the pub for me must be those big windows with their coloured glass. They are simple and yet, when the sun shines in to the pub, it picks out the yellow glass and is quite impressive. That said, I will leave you to make your own judgement on the light fittings and the very big framed mirrors which dominate one of the rooms.

They do, I suppose, remind me that, once, some pubs fell over themselves to market glitter and grandeur, marking them out as a direct contrast to the more drab homes of

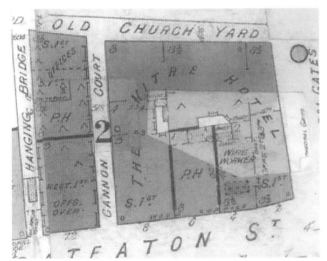

Mitre Hotel circa 1880s

many of their customers, and, for some, they rivalled the cinemas of the first few decades of the 20th century, which, in their way, were equally palaces of magic and entertainment.

The Crown and Anchor...
which flirted with Mr Chester's Pie and Ale House.

Today, the Crown and Anchor takes up a stretch of Cateaton Street, having expanded into one of the neighbouring premises. There has been a pub on the site since the 18th century and various breweries have run the place. Briefly, it changed from

Crown & Anchor 1970

the Crown and Anchor and became Mr. Chester's Pie and Ale House but has reverted to its old name, which is all to the good.

Now, as we have seen, many of our pubs have regularly changed their names, which is part fashion, part marketing ploy and most simply down to the whim of the landlord.

So, had you carried on down into Salford along Chapel Street, you would have come across the Rover's Return which until quite recently was the Lord Nelson. Its name was changed as a mark of respect to that long running

soap based on the fictional Weatherfield which everyone associates with Manchester, but in reality was Salford. That said, the same back streets could be found across both of the twin cities and out across the rest of the north and into the Midlands.

I still like Tony Warren's original name Florizel Street but can see how Coronation Street was a better choice.

As for the Rover's Return, there was one on the Manchester side of the river not far from the Crown and Anchor, but it vanished a long time ago, which just leaves me to say I for one am pleased that the name Mr. Chester's Pie and Ale House was ditched in favour of the old one.

And after a decent stay in the pub, you might just want to take in something of what this bit of the city has to offer, which of course has to begin with the Cathedral. There are plenty of good histories of this building, and in searching for them you will have to go inside, which leaves me to reflect on some of the other things worth noting.

Just down Cateaton Street, there are fine views across into

Salford and the site of the old Exchange Railway Station. Parts of the station approach and surrounding area were, for years, a car park, but have now been transformed, and the beauty of this book is that, whenever you buy it, the station site will certainly have changed.

Crown & Anchor (Browns Butchers) 1906

As I write, builders are there having cleared the site and soon construction work will begin.

As far as railway stations go, it lacked the style of Victoria railway station which is just a short walk away. Victoria is all that you would expect of a railway station. The exterior consists of an elegant stone building fronted with a fine glass and iron canopy, which still retains the destinations that the late Victorian traveller could access from its platforms. Added to this, there are two fine war memorials, a fascinating mosaic, and that new roof.

Now, you can either catch the tram from Exchange Square, which in one short ride will take you into the station, or alternatively you can walk it via Shambles Square, down the side of the Cathedral into the Gardens and then passing the entrance to Chethams School, arrive at Victoria Station Approach.

DEANSGATE

Rylands Library is well worth a visit not just for its architecture and books.

Deansgate

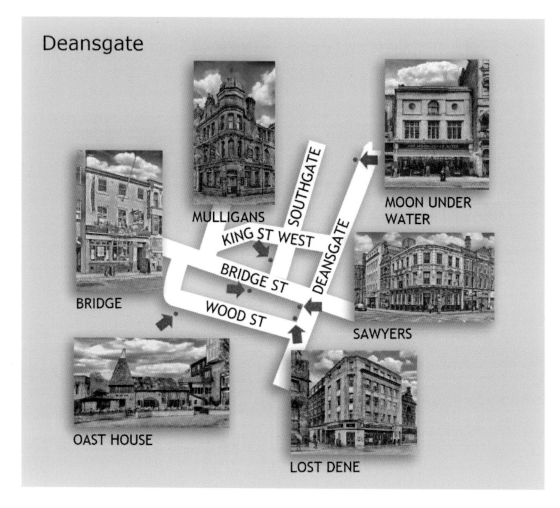

MULLIGANS

SOUTHGATE

DEANSGATE

KING ST WEST

BRIDGE ST

WOOD ST

BRIDGE

MOON UNDER WATER

SAWYERS

OAST HOUSE

LOST DENE

That long road from St Mary's Gate down to Knott Mill, with the lots of impressive buildings, some notable historic pubs, a Roman fort and the first passenger railway station.

Deansgate is a very long road and is best done in short walks, but never forget that at the end of it is a heap of history, including that Roman fort, the first passenger railway station, the Duke's Canal and the Beetham Tower.

In the 19th century, bits of it were notorious for its poor housing, its dangerous alleys and even darker courts, which only the brave or foolhardy entered unless you had no choice.

All of that has long gone and, instead, the carefree tourist is presented with a mix of shopping pleasure and a dollop of culture. It begins with that building opposite the Moon Under Water which is home to the Burlington Arcade. This is our only surviving Victorian shopping centre and contains some fine ironwork, some interesting shops and that beautiful glass entrance best seen from St Ann's Square.

A littler further down Deansgate and entered by St Marys Street is Parsonage Gardens whose tranquillity hides a violent episode when a King and Church mob laid siege to the home of the radical Thomas Walker who had upset the crowd by supporting the French Revolution. The day was only saved when Mr. Walker discharged a pistol and the crowd vanished like snow in the winter sun.

And for those who revel in fiendish pub questions there is a link between Thomas Walker, Mrs. Rylands and the big library which bears the family name just a short walk along Deansgate. The answer is not, I hasten to add in the Rylands Library, which is well worth a visit because of its architecture and books. Nor am I going to tell you the link, other than that the very respected Mr. Walker was put on trial for conspiracy during the French Revolution and that Mrs. Rylands was adamant that there should be no statue of her displayed in the Library.

As for the library, it really is pretty much like walking through a cathedral and it is very easy to get lost while wandering through the small rooms.

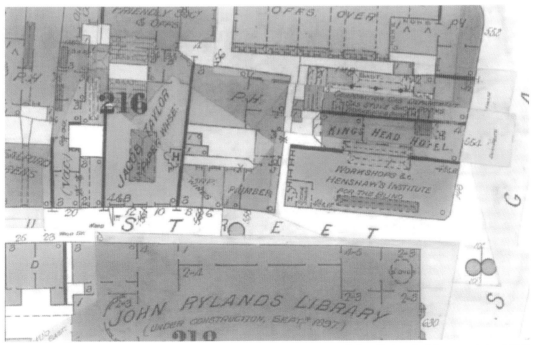

John Rylands Library circa 1880

The Moon Under Water...
once a cinema which closed in 1990.

If you are on the wrong side of 30, you will remember the Moon Under Water as a cinema. It opened in 1914, could seat 1,500 and, according to the Manchester Guardian, "was crowded all the afternoon and evening", and, unlike the Variety

Moon Under Water (ABC) 1976

Theatres, "there was no waiting outside [and there] was the added advantage of going in when you like and of being able to see the complete performance, with smoking permitted and babies in arms not forbidden".*

All of which made it one of the most popular city centre picture houses and it remained so after the addition of a second screen in 1971 which was carved out of the former cafe. Sadly, it closed in 1990 which means that, when I go in, I do have to bite back the nostalgia when remembering this was where we saw Shaft and heaps of other iconic movies of the period.

That said, it is hard to place myself back in that big dark room watching the flickering images, and that is down to the interior of the pub which is bright and ornate with all that gilt, coloured glass and carved balustrade. But that does offer up continuity with the old cinema. In the days

before the multiplex and even the division of cinemas into two studios, picture houses were magical places. In the 1960s many still retained that elegance that made them special.

It started with the walk down the road and spotting the cinema in the distance all lit up in a way few other buildings would have been at the time. Then there was the fact that you had to queue outside, standing in different lines depending on the choice of seats constantly guarded by the uniformed cinema employee, kitted out with a peaked cap, and jacket displaying gold braid and the badge of the cinema chain picked out on his shoulder.

The uniforms extended to the staff in the ticket booth, and the usherettes who saw you to your seats and who later would be there in the interval in front of the big screen selling choc ices, ice cream and those impossible sweet orange drinks. And, just occasionally talking to the customers in the most expensive seats, would be the manager in his dark formal suit with starched white shirt and bow tie.

Moon Under Water (ABC) 1962

All of which was just the overture to a night of fun excitement and, depending on your age and luck, a little bit of romance on the back row.

Of all the memories many of us will retain of those old picture palaces, it is probably the smell of the auditorium mixed with the warmth and the lush thick carpets and equally plush curtains.

This was grand entertainment and on a wet cold night there was nothing better.

More so, if the alternative was a mean flat with a threadbare carpet, a sad looking gas fire and the smell of stale cabbage from upstairs, so next time I am in the Moon Under Water, I rather think I will reflect over my pint on the relative merits of the film Cleopatra and those enamel stripping fruit drinks which were impossible to open.

*Picture Theatres in Manchester, Manchester Guardian, April 14, 1914

Mulligans...

some people will know it as The Wagon and Horses.

Now it is easy to miss Mulligans on Southgate which is a bit off the beaten track and so, unless you have been told about the place, it is a pub you fall across by accident.

And that is how we discovered it by sheer chance in 1972, probably after having seen a film at the ABC on Deansgate which long ago became the Moon Under Water. Back then, Mulligans was the Wagon and Horses and for me was at its best in the very early evening when the crowd was a mix of those stopping off for a quick drink after work and the first wave of those coming in for a night in town.

In the space between the working day and the evening, a sort of quiet stillness descended in anticipation of the night ahead, matched by the different groups in the pub. The shop workers and clerical staff were subdued but relaxed, and were at odds with the more boisterous and edgy customers who were hoping for a promising evening.

It would be a full four decades before I wandered back down Southgate looking for the Wagon and Horses and it took me sometime to realize that it had become Mulligans. In much the same way I doubt that Mr. John Travis landlord of the Wagon and Horses in 1851 would recognise what they had done to where he lived.

Today, the pub faces the back of a building, but, back in the 1850s, from his front door he would have looked out on to the Deansgate Shambles, which also stretched down past his pub.

Within a year, our old

Mulligans (Wagon & Horses) 1970

friend Mr. Adshead the cartographer would record that the Shambles had changed its name to the Bridge Street Market and incorporated

the Deansgate Arcade Market specializing in fruit and vegetables.

And if that were not enough, soon even the surrounding streets would have a makeover which would mean an end to New Shambles, which became the continuation of Southgate, and the loss of Pork Lane leaving only Butter Lane to survive into the 21st century, and in that bonfire of old names and places also went the delightfully named, Pork and Carcase Market which stretched from New Shambles to Butter Lane.

But while the names may have changed something of the narrow and twisty nature of the roads has survived, so after you leave the pub, make your way down Back Bridge Street which is as narrow as you get, and allows you to either take a

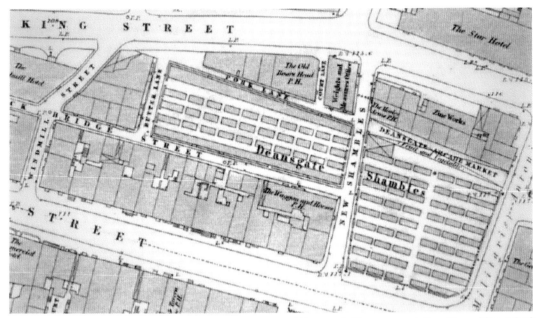

Wagon & Horses and the Shambles 1849

sharp right into Butter Lane or continue on, before opening up on to Motor Street Square, which technically is not a square and as far as I know has no official name.

The Bridge (The Pack Horse) 1970

The Bridge...

known as Goblets Wine Bar in the seventies when wine bars were the height of sophistication.

The Bridge is another of those pubs that a time traveller heading forward from some point in the middle of the 19th century might have difficulty in recognising. It's not so much the building as its name. Back in 1850 it was the Pack Horse Tavern then dropped the "Tavern" sometime before 1911 and later became the Bridge Street Tavern before briefly taking the title of Goblets Wine Bar when that first fashion wave for wine bars spread through the city centre in the 1970s. And there is

another fascinating discovery which is linked to the way that alleys, streets and even entries are preserved while all around them major redevelopments tear down old buildings and replace them with new.

The covered entry that leads from Wood Street to the yard of the Pack Horse pub is just such an example. If you go looking for the entry, the chances are that you will miss it because, for certain parts of the day and night, the entry is closed off by a door which you might just assume is one of the

doors that leads into the Wood Street Mission.

And if you went looking for the Pack Horse Yard you won't find that either. The Pack Horse, or the Free Mason's Tavern as it was sometimes called, was on Bridge Street.

The building is still there, but now goes under the name of the Bridge which, given its location on Bridge Street, makes perfect sense.

It's a long thin place and at the back there is a door into the yard; go through the yard and you will enter a tiled passage way which leads out onto Wood Street.

For those who like just a bit of atmosphere, the yard also has an old fashioned lamp post. The passageway was there in the 1790s and it seems that successive building development included it in the layout of new properties, and the Wood Street Mission which still occupies the site was no different.

The Bridge Inn 1959

The Oast House...

just a stone's throw away from the People's History Museum.

You can't really miss the Oast House. It sits in the newly refurbished Crown Square which was once a rather dismal open space surrounded by Council offices and flanked by the Law Courts.

There were benches there, but you would be pushed to want to linger on one of them and I rarely saw anyone availing themselves of the opportunity to stare across the flagged area with its bits of weed, grass and windblown litter.

But the Oast House has added something quirky to this bit of Spinningfields which is all glass and steel buildings; you will either see it as a welcome diversion from all this twenty-first century architecture or think someone left it there by mistake, but there is no denying that it offers a range of really good beer, has one of those "interesting" mix of customers and is just fun.

Car Park and Gardens 1961

For those with a desire to extend their knowledge, just a short walk away on Left Bank in Spinningfields is the People's History Museum, part of which is in the former Edwardian pumping station and the rest in a stunning new building with views across the river to Salford. The museum contains displays on local and national working-class life including a collection of trade union banners. They

come in all sizes but most are big and if you have ever had to carry one in a stiff wind with the rain coming down, you'd know it is, at best, a challenge. And I suppose that is why many of

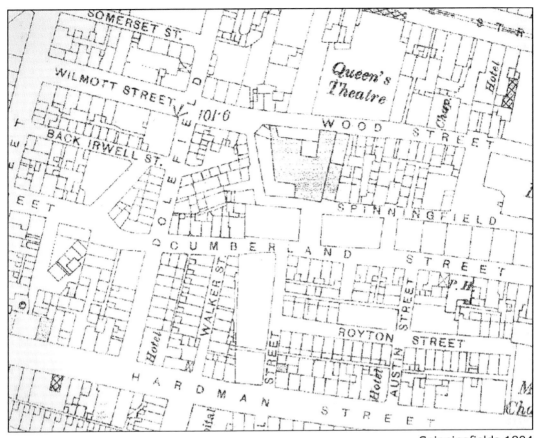

Spinningfields 1894

them after a century and a bit need some tender loving care and attention, which the museum offers in abundance.

For those with a sense of geography but who are a tad lazy, the balcony of the museum allows you to look down on the river, and the Mark Addy which was named after a hero of Salford. The Mark Addy is well worth a visit, allowing the interested and curious to compare it with both the Oast House and the Lost Dene.

The Lost Dene...

how many have eaten Chinese food here when it was The Willow Garden?

The Lost Dene fascinates me, not least because of its location. Back at the start of the last century, the site was occupied by the "Outdoor workshops of Henshaws Institute for the Blind" and the Kings Head Hotel and in 1850 this was the site of a group of shops, houses and workshops, all of which makes the Lost Dene a most modern pub and indeed, until recently, it was the Hogshead. But for some of us it will always be the Willow Garden, which served some amazing Chinese food and after its demise was briefly a showroom for office equipment.

Like all city centre Chinese restaurants, it offered a three course business meal for just 3 shillings at midday. I was always a fan of the business meal and especially of the custard which was always as bright yellow as a day glow poster and so

The Lost Dene (Woodhouse) 1938

sweet that you could almost imagine the sugar acting on the enamel of your teeth.

But the restaurants were not to the liking of everyone. I

well remember the niece of the landlady I once stayed with being most disparaging about the restaurants. It wasn't the food or the service it was rather that, as she said in a conspiratorial way, "Have you ever

noticed that they were always downstairs and underground".

I can't say I had, but I suppose the rent was cheaper and big old cellars below offices allowed for more tables and a freedom of layout.

Not so the Willow Garden, which was on ground level and sported a large silk and water colour panel of a willow tree, which I rather think also had coloured glass set into it.

If you tired of that, there was always the cafe next door, which in addition offered dance classes on the floor above and was also home to the Birdcage Club. It went under the grand name of

The Lost Dene (Woodhouse) 1938

the Magnet Restaurant. The building is still there between the Lost Dene and the Sawyers Arms but the Bird Cage and Dance school have long gone.

As for the Lost Dene, on the day we were there it was full of passing trade, most of whom had slipped in during a bout of holiday shopping.

Sawyers Arms...

it hasn't always had that glazed brick and tile appearance.

I first went in the Sawyers Arms on the corner of Bridge Street and Deansgate in the early 1970s. I suppose I was attracted by its distinctive red, yellow and cream glazed tiled frontage.

Now, over forty years later, I have no memory of what it looked like inside, but I guess that, back then, it was still divided up into small rooms, allowing people to create their own private little retreat with a few intimate friends. Not that there is anything of that left today, which is a shame for a pub which can claim to have been serving its customers since 1771.

My own real interest in the place stems from its connection with Chorlton and the Cope Family. Frederick Cope described himself as a spirit and wine merchant and was in partnership

with his brother and they had a number of 'premises' across the city including the Sawyers Arms. Their connection with the Sawyer's Arms seems a short one, although they did continue their wine business well into the 19th century.

There will be plenty of people like me who have fond memories of the place, but none who will remember its makeover in the early 20th

The Sawyers Arms 1970

century, when it was given its current glazed brick and tile appearance by the Manchester Brewery Company who also did the Castle and the Turks Head.

And if you want another twisty alley story, the Sawyers offers up another one.

It was Stuart, who runs the pub, who first told me about the passageway which navigates the back of the pub, and so, as ever an adventurous soul, I was off down Bridge Street to find it, and sure enough there it was.

The entry is unnamed and leads down towards Hollins Chambers which was built in 1925, and then, as mysterious and intriguing alleys go, it takes a left turn and then a right before coming out on Wood Street.

As you would expect, it is pretty much like walking through a canyon and with nothing but the walls of the surrounding buildings rising from street level, but here the history comes into play, because once, a little over a century and a bit ago, the entry never got as far as Wood Street and so, had you walked the walk back in 1851, your journey would have ended in a series of closed courtyards which also gave access to the back of the Sawyers Arms and another pub called the Old Bulls Head. To be fair, you did get close to Wood Street, but your journey would have come up against a dead end.

The intriguing question is when was that last section opened up, and it seems to have been sometime before 1894, but why this was so I have yet to discover.

In the meantime, I shall end with that fine looking building, Hollins Court, which stands in the alley just off Bridge Street.

Before it went up in 1925, this had been the site of yet another pub, which variously went under the name of the Cheshire Tavern, and the Cheshire Cheese, but had gone by 1911.

If you want to explore the passage way, it can be entered from Bridge Street, or, if you have a mind, by plunging down Wood Street and looking for that entrance.

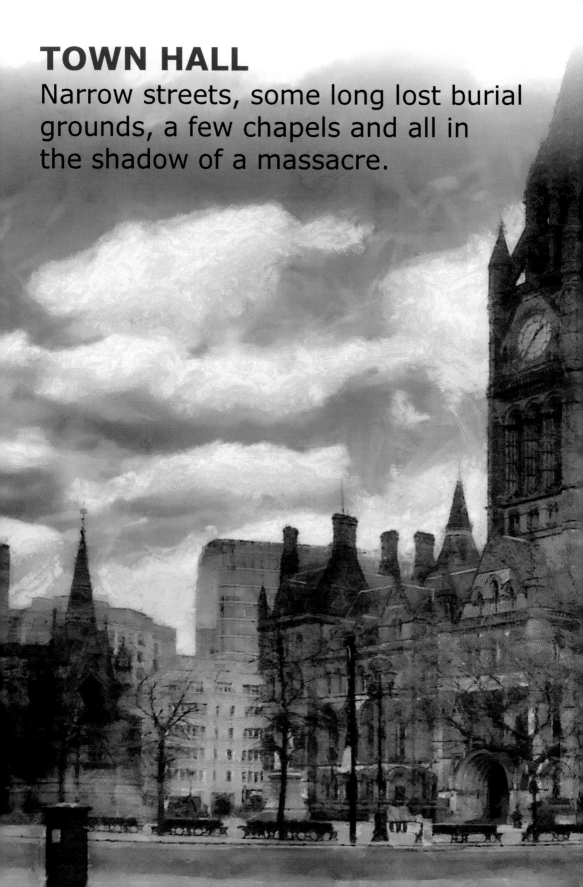

TOWN HALL

Narrow streets, some long lost burial grounds, a few chapels and all in the shadow of a massacre.

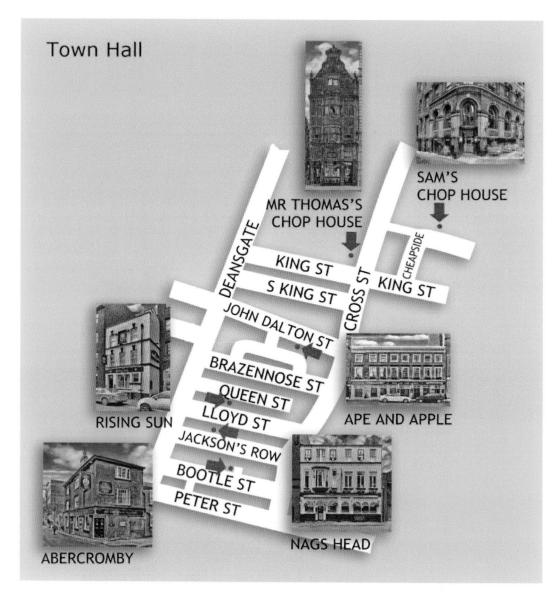

Town Hall

MR THOMAS'S CHOP HOUSE

SAM'S CHOP HOUSE

DEANSGATE

KING ST

S KING ST

CROSS ST

KING ST

CHEAPSIDE

JOHN DALTON ST

BRAZENNOSE ST

QUEEN ST

LLOYD ST

RISING SUN

APE AND APPLE

JACKSON'S ROW

BOOTLE ST

PETER ST

ABERCROMBY

NAGS HEAD

Now, you might be forgiven for doubting that, stretching north from Bootle Street, our walk would take in several vanished burial grounds which can still offer up some nasty surprises, a clutch of chapels like the New Jerusalem Church and the Friends Meeting House and dark alleys with names like Seyer's, Court Roger's Row and South Sea.

But take the walk and some of the evidence for those lost burial places and chapels is still there to see, although much has gone, from Brignal's Dyes Works, Sandbach's Tanyard and the site of the Corporation's Fire Engine & Scavenging Department.

Many of these would have been familiar to the crowds who piled into the city on an August day in 1819 to hear "Orator Hunt" and others put the case for Parliamentary reform.

They had walked in from the surrounding towns, some led by bands like the Stalybridge Brass Band, and here they joined the thousands from Manchester who turned out in holiday mood and in expectation of a rousing meeting.

It all turned out very differently after the mounted militia had charged into the packed crowds at St Peter's Field leaving some dead and many wounded.

The memory of those events and relics from the day stayed with many of those who had been there and were passed on to succeeding generations, from blood soaked clothing to bits of the banners which had been proudly carried into the field, and a full sixty five years later, a group of Peterloo veterans posed for a photograph taken by Mr. John Birch who surrounded the men and women with contemporary posters calling for reform.

The impact of that day was felt way beyond the city centre. Out on the southern side of Manchester in the rural heartlands of Chorlton-cum-Hardy and Didsbury, farmers referred to the "radical potato" which they grew. It had gained its name because of Mr. Johnson of Northenden, who grew and sold the "radical" and had been imprisoned for being on the platform calling for parliamentary reform.

Jackson's Row 1849

Sir Ralph Abercromby...

down Bootle Street with a ghost and a soldier.

You can approach Bootle Street from either Deansgate or from the back of Central Ref on Mount Street, but either way, you will be plunged into one of those narrow thoroughfares which, with just a little bit of imagination, takes you back to the early 19th century. Half way along is the pub, which takes its name from one of those distinguished servants of the Crown who combined a military career with that of being a politician from 1758 till his death in 1801, from wounds he incurred at the Battle of Alexandria.

All of which is interesting enough, but equally fascinating is the fact that he sided with the American colonists in the War of Independence. Sadly for some at least, it is not his memory that sits behind the bar but an unknown person who was killed at Peterloo when the militia charged into the crowds in August 1819.

The story of how his ghost occupied the building is possibly less interesting than that directly opposite was the

Abercrombie Inn 1946

New Jerusalem Church which extended back on to Peter Street, or that behind the pub on part of Jacksons Row and

Deansgate was the Quaker's Burial Ground. This last resting place of some of the good and pious long ago disappeared under a succession of

buildings of which 201 Deansgate is but the most recent.

But for the curious there is still a tiny piece of what was once Bottle Alley which ran from Deansgate giving access to the dark and dismal courts of Munday Square and Royle's Court which between them accounted for nineteen back to back cottages.

And for those emboldened by an evening in the Sir Ralp Abercromby, there is just a hint of that long vanished alley in the space between 201 Deansgate and the neighbouring restaurant. It advances no more than a few paces before an iron gate bars the way and ends in an open space. But you had better be quick because there are plans to redevelop the area and, like all development plans, beside the new and shiny there will be casualties.

One of these may well be the Abercromby. The developers are keen to replace the pub with another, thereby saving jobs but I doubt it will be the same, so, armed, or should I say forewarned by this news, the dedicated beer drinker along with the historian should spend some time down there. After all it is a pleasant place with fine wooden bars and some interesting carved panels.

Abercrombie Inn 1950s

The Old Nags Head...

The Nags Head is one of those pubs most of us find by chance.

You take a short cut from Deansgate up towards Albert Square and there it is.

That said, it does offer up a second opportunity to find it, because it has another entrance on Lloyd Street which runs parallel to Jackson's Row. This second entrance is less impressive than the first so we shall stick with Peter's painting which captures the place from Jackson's Row on a bright summer's day.

It is what you would expect of an old city centre pub but the dates on the wall obscure the fact that it was open for business by 1824, and maybe even earlier.

In 1824 Charles Vale was pulling the pints and a little later a James Wood, not that either would have recognised the pub today or indeed Jackson's Row.

Back then and into the next few decades this was one of those typical Manchester streets fronted by houses which in turn hid dark courts of smaller properties, which were accessed

Old Nags Head 1970

along narrow passageways, opening into closed, almost secret areas where few but the residents went.

And to add to the gloom, the immediate area was dominated

by factories, a tannery and a handful of timber and coal yards.

Still, there was one bit of open land on the corner of Jackson's Row and Deansgate which might have afforded a place to sit for a few minutes, but, given that this was the Quaker's Burial Ground, I doubt that it was much of an attraction and anyone wanting a bit of cheer was forced back in the Nags Head in the middle of the Row, or The Far Tavern opposite the burial ground, with the option of visiting the Coach Makers Arms at the other end of the street hard by the coach factory.

I first fell across the Old Nags Head back in the early 70s and was intrigued by the coffin in the rear of the pub, which is another story for another time and will lead me to that now lost pub Tommy Ducks.

In the meantime, I wish I had been old enough to drink in there when the likes of Judy Driscoll, Long John Baldry, Rod Stewart and Brian Auger of the "Steampacket" regularly rehearsed upstairs in the blue room before performing in the

old Twisted Wheel.

It was one of a number of colourful stories that Sean the landlord was happy to recount along with tales of its time as a "Mod pub" and more recently as a meeting up place once a year for servicemen attending the service at the Cenotaph.

Old Nags Head 1971

Rising Sun...
the pub that faces two ways.

Now not everything is as it seems when you sit in the Rising Sun. First, there is that notable fact that it is one of the few pubs in the city centre where you can enter by one street and leave by another. The grander of the two sides is the Queen Street entrance with its distinctive gold sun that is set in blue stone at the top of the pub and the equally impressive gold lettering.

Rising Sun 1971

But as late as 1911 there was only the one entrance on Queen Street and the rear on Lloyd Street was a different premises, listed that year as an electrical business. And nor is that all, because this part of Lloyd Street was still known in the 1860s as Back Queen Street and that car park beside the pub was once the playground of St Ann's Church School.

Of course there is always a hiccup in the flow of historical

narrative and, despite all the evidence that the Rising Sun was a smaller place, Mr. Adshead's map dated 1850 has it facing

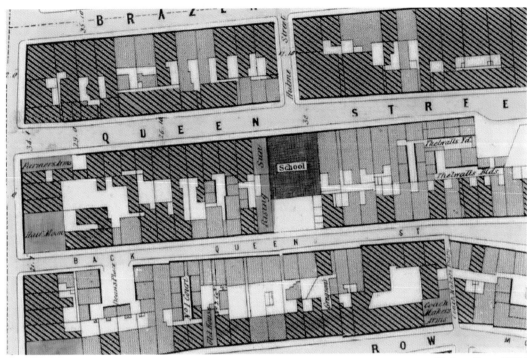

Rising Sun 1851

out on both Queen Street and Back Queen Street.

All of which is enough to drive anyone to order another pint.

The Ape and Apple...
home to Lambert and Smith Solicitors in 1969

Now I can remember almost to the day when I discovered the Ape and Apple on John Dalton Street. For years, the presence of the Habitat store on the corner with Ridgefield was what drew me down the street, along with the little ginnel, beside New Church House, which led on to Tasle Alley and by degrees, through the tunnel to Mulberry Street and St Mary's Chapel, which is more popularly known as the Little Gem.

Not having wandered down there for years when I came across the place which opened in the 1990s, I had to think very hard whether this had always been there or was new.

Ape and Apple (Manchester Exchange Bank) 1910

It is of course relatively new, for when I first walked past the building in 1969 it was home to Lambert and Smith Solicitors at number 28, the Solicitors Law Stationery Society Ltd and Oyez Office Furniture at numbers 28/30.

However, the interior has a charm about it which includes those big old easy chairs you associate with your gran's house. And I had to confess I went looking for those special head covers called antimacassars which were essential in those days when all men used Brylcreem or equivalent hair oil.

Nana was most strict about the use of those covers. Not so Mrs. Green next door who with four grown sons was forever lamenting the oily stains which long ago had sunk

deep into the armchairs. But neither had gone the next step of covering all the easy chairs and settee with those transparent plastic covers which I hated. Within ten minutes of sitting on

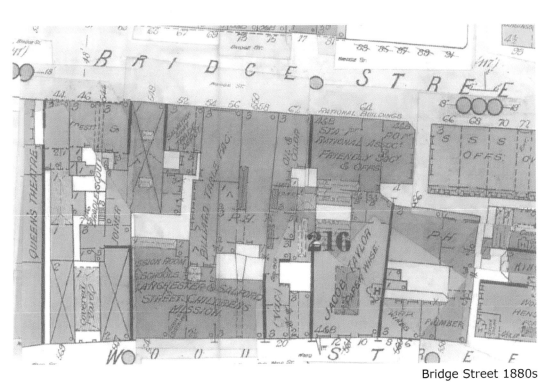
Bridge Street 1880s

one, your bottom had warmed through and there was that ever present danger that you would slowly slide off the seat.

Mr Thomas's...

not just a place to eat and drink but somewhere with class.

Mr Thomas's was opened in 1867 and you do get a sense that it has been on this bit of Cross Street forever.

I have only been going there since the early 1970s, but it is easy, as you sit in the restaurant, to conjure up images of sleek Edwardian businessmen eating oysters and drinking fine wines while discussing the day's work at the Exchange close by, or the odd carter calling in to celebrate the jubilee of the old Queen.

Part of that is because of its appearance.

It starts with those brown terracotta tiles on the outside of the building and continues inside with that mix of cream and green wall tiles. Added to which is the distinctive chequered floor tiles and the arched recess which acts as a gigantic wine rack.

Most of this dates from its makeover in 1901 when the place was extended. Since then the interior has been restored and is now a Grade II listed building, which is about all there is left to say save that one source asserts that the terracotta tiles were hand cast and delivered to the site hollow and then filled with concrete for extra strength and fabricated over the cast iron frame on site.

Not quite all to say, for, if you get yourself one of the seats by the front window, you can gaze out across Cross Street and ponder on the fate of some of those who were buried there.

It's one of those dark stories that had the engineers who were building the Metro Second City Crossing stop work on the discovery of human remains.

The bodies were of

Mr Thomas's Chop House 1970

those interred in the Cross Street Chapel and for some months, tents were pitched and work was done to unearth the remains.

But, and here I have to confess I can't remember the source, there is also an assertion that much of the land behind Mr Thomas's stretching out beyond St Ann's Church and into the square also has its fair share of graves resting peacefully below the ground. All of which

leaves me pondering on the nights and indeed the afternoons I have spent in the company of Mr Thomas.

Of all those many events, I suppose the one that stands out is the afternoon I entertained one of my Canadian friends who was on a whistle stop tour of the country. By the time we met up in Manchester, she had "done" Scotland, London, the West Country and only missed Wales because she missed a connection.

We had visited the Rylands, the Town Hall, Central Ref and even Media City and with a tram ride as well, it was time to offer Susan a "piece of period eating".

I could have chosen Sam's Chop House but in the end it was the tiled interior which tipped the scales in favour of Mr Thomas's, and I have to say that, for anyone

Mr Thomas's Chop House 1972

who has never been before, it has got the lot.

It starts with the outside of the building which looks as if it has been squeezed into a plot too small for its grand design. Then you go inside with the small bar tiled floor and panelled walls only to be met a minute later by the impressive dining area.

I never tire of the place and I know Susan will remember it fondly.

Sam's Chop House...

often frequented by L S Lowry.

Sam's is situated on the corner of Chapel Walks and Back Pool Fold, both of which might well puzzle the curious tourist. Back Pool Fold is one of those twisty little thoroughfares which you think must have a rich and varied history and at sometime have offered up more than a few dark stories, but for now it's the name that provides a clue to how this bit of the city has changed and it all hangs on the word "Back" which suggests there must once have been a Pool Fold and, sure enough, in the late 18th century there was.

Sam's Chop House 1973

It was the continuation of Cross Street, which in 1793 terminated at the corner with Chapel Walks leaving Pool Fold to creep up to Market Street past what was then the New Shambles. And as such would have been familiar to those Dissenters who attended the Cross Street Chapel, which dates from 1694 and which is the origin of the name Chapel Walks. There will be many who remember walking down Chapel Walks past the grassed area at the rear of the chapel and clocking that this was the site of the graveyard. It vanished under the last rebuild of the chapel in 1997, which is the fourth place of worship to occupy the site. The first was

opened in 1694, and destroyed by a mob in 1715; its successor succumbed to an air raid in December 1940, and the replacement built in 1959 survived for four decades.

Sam's Chop House cannot claim to have stood on its present site for that long, having opened at Back Fold Place in the 1950s, although it does date back to 1872 when Mr. Samuel Studd opened his restaurant under the grander name of Sam's London Chop House.

It was situated in Manchester Chambers on the corner of Market Street and Pall Mall.

The building has long gone, but, once and not that long ago, this corner was home to the UCP shop, which for those who don't know was the United Cattle Products Company which had a chain of 146 restaurants. You entered from that corner, went up a large staircase into the restaurant and there, amongst many cattle products on offer, was tripe.

We only went in once and never bothered with the pub next door on Pall Mall. It was called the Tavern and I can't say it looked inviting.

Chapel Walks from Cross Street towards Sam's Chop House 1914

There was one entrance, and the windows ran in a long strip high up on the wall. All of which may seem a long way from Sam's but I think not, for the connection may be L S Lowry who frequented the place and should have included a tripe shop in one of his paintings.

CITY ART GALLERY
And some equally interesting little pubs.

City Art Gallery

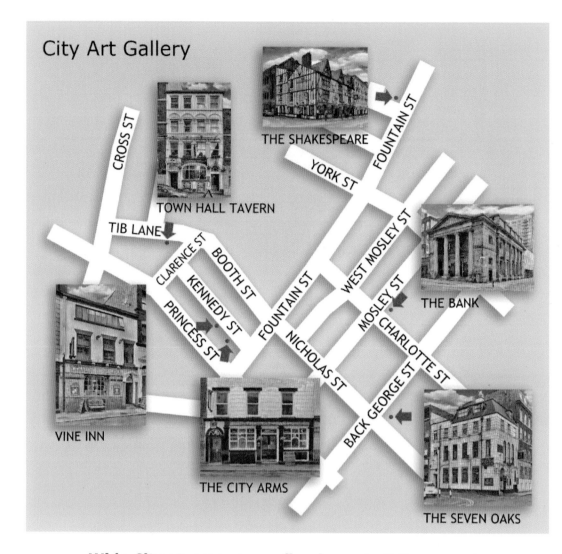

CROSS ST

THE SHAKESPEARE

FOUNTAIN ST

YORK ST

TOWN HALL TAVERN

TIB LANE

CLARENCE ST

BOOTH ST

KENNEDY ST

PRINCESS ST

FOUNTAIN ST

WEST MOSLEY ST

MOSLEY ST

THE BANK

NICHOLAS ST

CHARLOTTE ST

BACK GEORGE ST

VINE INN

THE CITY ARMS

THE SEVEN OAKS

Wide City streets, some fine large buildings, and some equally interesting little pubs.

Now we are entering one of those bits of the city which are a testimony to both Manchester's great commercial success and also the value it put in cultural and scientific pursuits. So just along Mosley Street is the Portico Library, opened in 1806 and paid for by 400 subscribers who each committed to subscribing 20 guineas.

According to Mr. Duffield in his excellent guide to Manchester published in 1850 "the Library boasted 14,000 volumes and the files of newspapers which are considered the best outside of London".*

All of which is just an introduction because, a little further down the road, is the City Art Gallery which dates from 1823, and just beyond the edge of the walk are the Town Hall and the Cenotaph.

But behind some of these fine buildings were a mix of meaner streets and plenty of those closed courts, and as these courts will feature heavily in this and surrounding walks this may be the time to reflect on what they were and what they were like.

The swift expansion of the city during the early decades of the 19th century offered builders, and especially speculators, a golden opportunity to build small, cheap and often poorly constructed homes for those who worked in the mills, iron works and other industries.

Many were one up one down, back to back properties and some were built in courts off a street which were accessed by a narrow alley. They were dark, even in the bright glare of a sunny day, and admitted little fresh air.

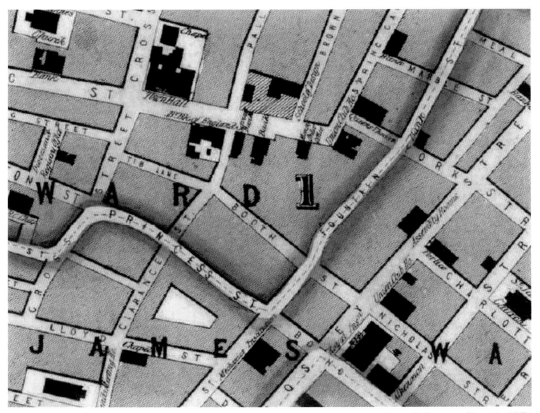

Princess Street 1851

*The Stranger's Guide to Manchester, H F Duffield

The Shakespeare...
with more than a few stories.

Fountain Street is one of those no nonsense streets which take you all the way from Market Street down almost to St Peter's Square crossing a number of busy roads along the way. For the curious tourist it also presents some opportunities to explore what were once the back alleys of the city.

One of these is Sickle Street which is approached from

The Shakespeare 1970

Fountain Street via Phoenix Street and which will still take you by a twisty route back to Market Street, although those closed courts which ran off the street are gone.

And that is possibly for the best because these were not to be investigated by anyone with money in their pockets. Today, it is still possible to follow the course of the street and like them find the way becoming progressively narrower. But for most people I suspect the attractions of the

Shakespeare will win over an adventure along what is really now just a glorified car park.

And here we must be careful of Eric, the man best described as the Nemesis of the naive. I first met him at a lecture on the history of Manchester pubs over thirty years ago and made that fatal mistake of catching his eye. Twenty minutes later I knew all there

was not to know about the older drinking places in the city.

I can't remember what claims he made for the Shakespeare, which was certainly offering pints by 1824 when Mr. Job Dikin was the landlord, and some sources suggest it was on Fountain Street by 1771. That said, at least one old map dating from 1772 shows that the street had yet to be cut.

Not that Mr. Dikin nor his predecessors would have recognised the timber frame exterior which actually came from Chester and, while it dates from the 17th century, did not make its appearance in the city until sometime in the 1920s.

Which just leaves the inevitable ghost story

which, in this case, involves a girl who was murdered by the chef who then took his own life by hanging himself and yep, there are those who claim to have seen the rope marks on a beam and yet other people who claim to have seen the ghostly appearance of the girl at the top of the stairs. Eric believes the story and has advanced the case for 1771, but I will remain a tad sceptical on both counts.

Town Hall Tavern...

just around the corner from The Town Hall.

The Town Hall Tavern on Tib Lane looks the part of one of our oldest pubs. It rises majestically over four floors and can still hold its own against its neighbours. It is best approached from Essex Street which is another of those narrow little streets that cover the area and, as you stroll up from King Street, the pub dominates the view with the added bonus of a fine glimpse of the Town Hall off to the left.

It was selling pints by 1824 and, given that the street was laid out and full of

The Town Hall Tavern 1970

buildings by 1772, I expect it will be older. And it has seen off

all its competitors, which at one point in 1850 included another pub and two beer shops in what was a street of just fifteen properties.

Today, there is the added attraction that the rear opens up on Bow Lane which must be one of the narrowest of thoroughfares and has never warranted any interest from those who compiled the lists of city residents.

The rest is best left to those who venture in, although I must confess to be fascinated by another pub which was the Tinplate Workers Arms at 95 Long Millgate. I came across it on the same list of pubs for 1824. It had vanished just thirty years later and no one seems to have bothered to record its story. And yes there is no connection - just a love of the name.

But for those that collect pub interiors instead of names, the Town Hall Tavern has just undergone a makeover. We were there two days before it was due to reopen, and I have to admit both Peter and I were hard pressed to see how it would happen given the confusion of tradesmen, electrical cables and

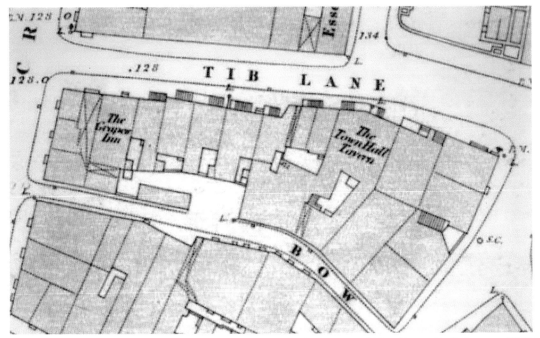

Tib Lane and The Town Hall Tavern 1849

unopened boxes of "things". But they did, and I rather think it
is an improvement on what I remember.

190

Vine Inn...

always stops the casual tourist in their tracks.

For many, the reward for the long walk along Fountain Street, which leads to Cooper Street is the Vine. It stands on Kennedy Street and is all green tiles and gold lettering. It remains one of those pubs you bring friends who are sniffy about Manchester and it always makes a huge impression.

Now I am sure someone will point to the long windows at the top and make the connection with handloom weavers' homes. Those top windows were designed to

Vine Inn 1970

admit the maximum amount of daylight. But if the house was occupied by a handloom weaver, he had gone by the 1850s, no doubt squeezed out by the growing mechanisation of the textile industry.

Instead, at number 46, Martha Dunbar was selling pints to the residents and passing trade in 1850, but by the following year had been replaced by Mr. Edwin Eastwood from Halifax in

Yorkshire. He and his wife were just 22 and I guess were an enterprising couple. They shared the house with Mr. and Mrs. Leach.

Next door at what is the City Arms was Mr. John

Turner at 48 who was also in the business of dispensing beer and happiness and both landlords were in direct competition with Alston William at number 36 and competition might well have been fierce given that there were 24 households along Kennedy Street whose breadwinners were engaged in a variety of trades from bookbinding, box manufacturer and my own personal favourite .... Mr. John Beswick, leech importer, who lived at number 9.

But selling beer was for many just a short term measure which helped overcome a short period of unemployment and had been made possible because the 1830 Beer Act allowed an individual to brew and sell beer for the price of a license costing two guineas.

And that is pretty much what seems to have happened on Kennedy Street; in the space of a year, not only had Mrs. Duncan moved on, but so had John Beswick at 48 whose place had been taken by a Mr. William who seems to have fancied selling beer rather than working as a blacksmith.

That said, many beer sellers retained their original occupations, seeing beer as just a side line.

All of which brings me back to the Vine which extended into the neighbouring building a few years ago and now features a cellar bar devoted to a range of interesting brands of whiskies.

I doubt very much if this is the building which Martha or the other publicans back in the 1850s would have known. It post-dates them and may have been built in the late 1870s when it was the offices of a solicitor, an accountant and a cloth agent.

These venerable and sober businessmen might well have shuddered at one story that Mike and Rachelle, the current owners of the Vine, told me about a Mary O' Sullivan who may have run the Vine at sometime in the past and may have been murdered in the little entry which once gave access from Kennedy Street into a courtyard behind the pubs.

The passage way, which was on the west side of the City Arms, was still there at the beginning of the 20th century, but alas has now gone.

A first sweep of the records has not revealed Mary O'Sullivan, but Rachelle was told by someone researching his family tree that his ancestor was connected with the Vine so I shall continue to go looking.

The City Arms...

a meeting place for all walks of life.

I have fond memories of the City Arms, which was a pub I spent many Friday nights in, after meetings at the Town Hall, and later still was somewhere I brought my sisters, up from London for a taste of a real pub.

In its time, it has been the haunt of local politicians, town hall staff and a band of loyal customers, and of all the landlords who have stood and called time at the end of the night, my interest has been drawn to Edwin and Eliza Eastwood from Yorkshire.

In 1851, they were both just 22 and I guess had not been in the city for long. They had married the year before in Halifax where Eliza had been born, and both came from families of inn keepers.

Edwin described himself as a beer seller and, as the pub does not feature in the list of pubs and taverns in 1850, I

City Arms 1970

rather think he was one of those hundreds of people who had taken advantage of the 1830 Beer Act which had allowed the brewing and sale of beer from a person's house for a small fee.

It was often a side line to supplement the family's income, but for some it led on to better things. In the case of Edwin and Eliza, this was to

be the St Ledger Hotel on King William Street in Blackburn where they were pulling pints and serving customers by 1871. Three decades later, Edwin, aged 72, had become a property agent and

lived in a comfortable looking terraced house in Granville Road. Nor is that quite the end of the story of young Edwin and Eliza, for in 1861 after they may have already moved off, Edwin was visiting Manchester and staying at the Wagon and Horses

on the corner of Southgate and Back Bridge Street. It was still the Wagon and Horses back in the 1970s and we often slipped in there for a quiet drink before going off to the cinema, but now it is Mulligans.

It was the perfect place for an early evening drink, with a few office workers and shop assistants passing the time before they went home and before the evening crowd came in.

Back then it was close to the Deansgate Shambles.

But all of that is quite properly another pub and another story.

The Seven Oaks...

how many would slide in here for spiritual refreshment.

There has been a pub carrying the name the Seven Oaks on Nicholas Street from at least 1824 when James Jones, the landlord, was perhaps very pleased that the pub sat just one street from the church of St James on Charlotte Street, with its possibilities of the odd worshipper calling for another form of spiritual refreshment.

And within thirty years, his successor, a Mr. William Jenkinson, could add to the church: the Union Club on the next corner, the Royal Institution directly opposite and, a little way back up Mosley Street, the Portico Library.

To be fair, how many of the members of these bodies would slide into the Seven Oaks on a Saturday night is unknown, but the pub has survived and now sports those distinctive glazed tiles and that motif of an oak tree.

Today, however, the discerning customers might plan their trip to coincide with a visit to the Art Gallery opposite which offers some fine paintings, along with exciting

Seven Oaks Hotel 1970

temporary displays, housed in a period building which sits nicely with its glass additions.

And having spotted the Pre-Raphaelite paintings, along with those atmospheric ones

of Manchester by Valette, of Oxford Road and Albert Square in 1910, it might well be time to return to the Seven Oaks.

I have to say that, when we went in, I did begin to reflect on how Mr. Valette would have set about recording what he saw.

It was a busy day and the place was crowded with a mix of people and the coloured glass behind the bar and the lighting made me think of one of those Edwardian gin palaces not so different from the sort Mr. Valette would have known.

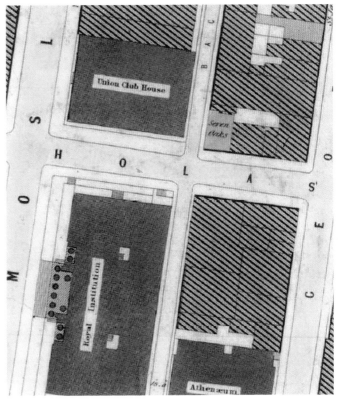

Seven Oaks 1851

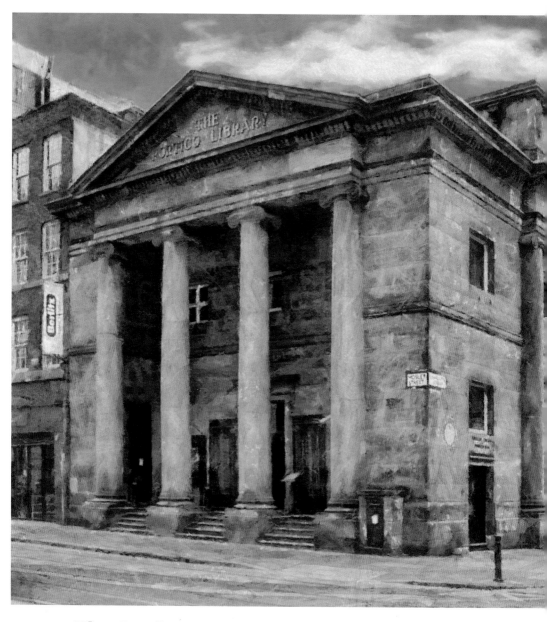

The Bank...

on Mosley Street completing the walk.

There will be those who shudder at the idea of a library dating back to 1806 becoming a pub, but if you have ever been invited into the Portico Library, which still occupies the upper floor of the building, you might concede it works.

The Library has elegance, with an air of serious learning which makes it easy to slip back two and bit centuries to when it was opened. It provided its subscribers with thousands of

The Bank (Portico Library) 1935

books as well as newspapers from across the country.

If you do get that invitation, just take advantage of one of the special exhibitions.

Alternatively, there is always the pub and, before anyone expresses sadness at the transformation, it is worth noting that the downstairs area, which was the Reading Room, was surrendered to a bank back in the 1920s and

remained so until relatively recently.

I rather like the grandeur of the interior, but, instead of writing about the décor, I will leave you with that Victorian pillar box which is fixed to the wall beside the Bank.

As we sipped a fine glass of the Bank's best I wondered how many

letters Mr. Ernest Marriot posted in that very pillar box.

He was the secretary and librarian of "the Portico Library and Newsroom", which predates our pillar box by some decades.

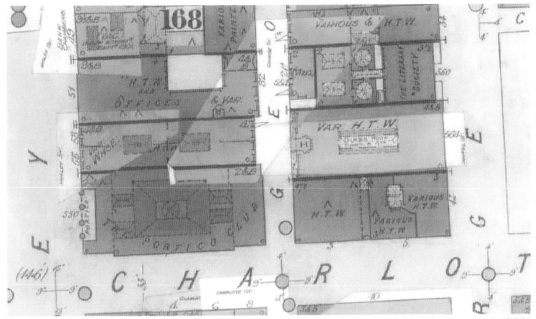

Portico Club Mosley Street circa 1880s

And unlike the Bank or the Library, our pillar box has not fared so well, having become a favourite for anyone wanting to stick an advertising label over its bright red surface.

I asked Peter to turn the post box into a painting and we debated whether to lose the stickers and scribble; in the interests of historical accuracy we kept them in. At which point I am sure someone will mutter, "we are not amused", given that this was one of the old Queen's post boxes.

But that would be to repeat a much misunderstood quotation from Queen Victoria, who apparently used it in the context of a rather drunken oaf who was making unfunny and obscene jokes at the dinner table.

Now, I have to confess I have never used the post box, but rather think it is time to do so. Peter tells me that he is minded to convert his painting into one of his picture postcards which I will then post to me from the box, and of course, on the way, slip back into the Bank.

PICCADILLY

A hospital, those gardens and
a walk beside the canal.

Piccadilly

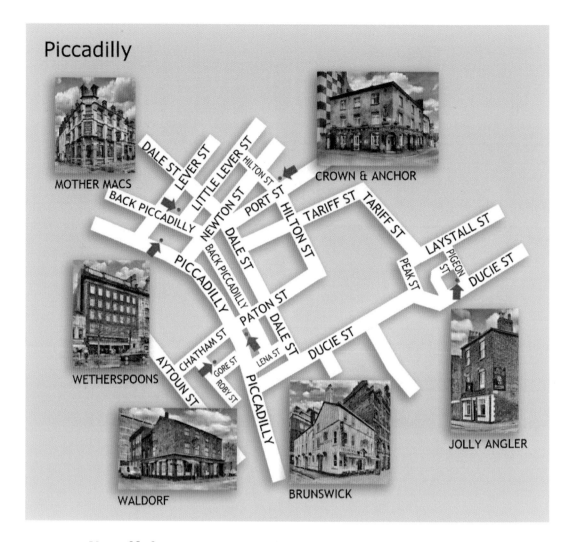

MOTHER MACS

CROWN & ANCHOR

WETHERSPOONS

JOLLY ANGLER

WALDORF

BRUNSWICK

Now if there are two things guaranteed to stir the pot, one is the closure of a hospital and the second is the remodelling of a much loved public park.

So before we embark on the walk which will take us from the Wetherspoons at no. 49 Piccadilly and by degrees down to the Jolly Angler by the Ashton Canal on Ducie Street, we should walk into Piccadilly Gardens.

In the Middle Ages, it was nothing more than a site used to excavate clay for building and was simply known as "daub holes", but in 1755 it became the home of the Manchester Royal Infirmary which continued to offer up medical care until 1910 when the hospital relocated to Oxford Road.

And then for the next twenty years the debate raged about what to do with this hole in the ground at the very centre of the city. And it was indeed a hole in the ground, which had been left over from the demolition of the old MRI, leading one journalist to comment, "the place has remained year after year a good imitation of a rubbish heap or the ruins of some volcanic upheaval".*

The proposals ranged from an Art Gallery, to a tramway terminus and an underground railway centre and, for a while, part of the site was occupied by Manchester's Reference Library. But, in 1920, the City Council decided to convert the site "into a pleasant garden. The existing hollow in the centre of the site is to be utilized for a sunken garden on the Dutch style and its banks will slope up to a border of flowering plants".*

And that is pretty much how it remained for almost eighty years before its makeover in 2001. That remodelling did and continues to excite a mix of opinions, many of which haven't been kind. For those wanting to cling to what once was a beautiful and popular spot in the heart of the city, there is just one bit of the old perimeter stone wall standing beside the metro line on the southwest corner of the gardens.

Of course, the area has undergone considerable redevelopment, partly as a result of the Manchester Blitz and then the development of the area in front of the bus station which, despite some recent modifications, is a good example of late 50s and early 1960s city build.

But that shouldn't blind us to the fact that Piccadilly and the route down London Road to Ducie Street has been constantly redeveloped as, first the Victorians, and then later early 20th century businessmen swept the past away in favour of the new.

And even before then the enterprising plans of industrialists and merchants paid scant regard to the open spaces and old buildings which vanished under warehouses, factories, a set of canals and a new railway, all existing beside a heap of houses some grander than others and some downright mean and shoddy.

Piccadilly Hotel 1939

*After Sixteen Years: A Garden For Piccadilly, Manchester Guardian, Oct 23, 1920

Wetherspoons on the right (Queen Victoria's Visit) 1851

Wetherspoons...
in the heart of Piccadilly.

Now, like most Wetherspoon pubs, you know that there will be a history to the place which is totally unconnected to beer, and this one is no exception. At the beginning of the last century, it was the proud premises of Chorlton Brothers Wholesalers who shared the building with Dean & Dawson Ltd who specialized in "excursions", and the Manchester and County Bank.

The Chorlton Brothers had their factory just behind on the corner of Newton Street and Back Piccadilly, and no doubt were pleased with the position of the showroom in Piccadilly, and may have banked with Manchester and County Bank which had begun in 1862 across the city at

Aerial view 1930

York Street. This became by degrees the District Bank, the National Provincial Bank and finally the National Westminster Bank.

All of which just leaves Mr. Dean and Dawson, who not only sold excursions but advertised themselves as tourist agents, with another branch on London Road, which was very handy for the railway station.

I doubt there is anything left of their time at no. 49, but just possibly there might be the odd casual visitor to the pub who remembers a lucky day back in the summer of 1968, when part of the building was the bookmakers, Seymour & Story and, having walked away with that successful bet, chose to celebrate with a Chinese meal in the Man Fang restaurant, followed by a visit to Burton's the Tailors which were both also located in number 49.

Of course, today, if you visit at lunchtime, the place seems full of people spending an hour or so over a pint and a meal.

Wetherspoons in the distance 1953

Mother Mac's...

stories of murders and ghosts.

You might be forgiven for thinking that Back Piccadilly is one of those long narrow thoroughfares that time has pretty much forgotten, and which is rarely visited and even more rarely talked about.

It stretches from Lena Street down to Tib Street and crosses three of the main routes out towards the north of the city and also gives access to another five streets which run off into Dale Street, yet walk its length and there is little to see. Most of the stretch consists of the back of properties which have their more public face on Dale Street or Piccadilly. But not quite, because just roughly half way along on the corner with Little Lever Street is Mother Mac's which was at one time called the Wellington.

Given that on a dark winter's night it might seem the only welcome sign of life along the entire length of

Mother Macs (Wellington Inn) 1970

Back Piccadilly, it should not be missed.

Of course you may want to forgo the story of the gruesome murder which reputedly took place inside, particularly if you are planning to walk back along the street later in

the night. It's a story which could probably be added to with others given that the pub has been dispensing beer and cheer for at least a century and a half.

But if you are looking for ghosts, my money would be on the barrow boys who may have finished off a day's trading with a couple of pints and who occupied Back Piccadilly selling everything from fruit and dried flowers to costume jewellery, toy mice and pretty much what ever would catch the punter's eye on a Saturday.

According to one journalist writing in 1961, "the shopping public, crowd each Saturday into the narrow canyon of Back Piccadilly to buy or just waste a minute listening to the eruptions of verbal slapstick" from the two dozen barrow boys.

At one end was the man with a three foot long barrage balloon which he flirted around his head accompanied by the cry "only a Bob. All best rubber and all that jazz", while his companion wooed the crowd with the latest continental jewellery shouting "C'mon darlin' dangle them from your ears and you'll look like the Queen of Sheba".*

Some claimed that their families, stretching back to their great grandfathers, had been working the pitches, but were fearful of new regulation which would drive them out.

And now they are no more, unlike the pub which has seen off its rivals which, at the beginning of the last century, included a Yates's Wine Lodge at the Oldham Street corner and the Merchants' Hotel. Back then, there were also forty

Mother Macs (Wellington) 1967

other businesses, all employing thirsty workmen and ensuring there were customers for all three.

All of which was perhaps easier than when the 77 year old James Grindrod managed the Wellington in 1851 and competed with The Mosley Tap Room, the Albion Tap Room and two other

beer retailers, at a time when Back Piccadilly consisted of just 22 properties.

After a short closure it has reopened after a makeover with one visitor commenting, "took me about half an hour to get used to the new, but still old fashioned ambience".

*Back Piccadilly may lose barrow Boys, the Manchester Guardian, November 20, 1961

Crown and Anchor...
noise and industry means thirsty workers.

Standing outside the Crown and Anchor on Hilton Street, you will get a very good lesson in the ups and downs of being a developer.

It starts with the grand plan, moves on to the careful attention to detail, making sure there is a mix of public and private properties, balanced by all the services needed for civilized life and then, when all seems to be going the right way, a set of unexpected events pretty much scuppers it all.

So it was for Mr. William Stevenson whose grand plan was to develop the area north of Piccadilly with a grid of streets varying in width, which would accommodate a variety of town houses all designed to appeal to the middle class, attracted by the open countryside which lay just beyond the development. At the centre of it all would be the grand square bounded by Lever Street to the east and Hilton Street to the west, which took his name.

Crown & Anchor 1961

Work was well under way by the early 1780s with the construction of new churches, including St Clements on the south side of Stevenson Square which was opened in 1793, but

those fields were perfect for the construction of the Rochdale and Ashton Canals which terminated at the bottom of Hilton Street, and with the canals came the textile factories, iron works and timber yards, along with the modest and often mean rows of workers cottages.

All of which meant that when Mr. Thomas Bake was handing out pints inside the Crown and Anchor in the January of 1824, Mr. Stevenson's vision of middle class life on the edge of the city had been overtaken. Fast forward another quarter of a century, and, within just a minute's walk from the pub, the sound of bird song was overwhelmed by the noise of the Newton Street Iron Works, the Iron Warehouse, the Small Ware Mill and umpteen factories given over to metal working, cotton spinning, and wood manufacture.

All of which would have been music to the ears of Thomas Ogden who was in charge of the Crown by 1850 and his fellow four beer retailers on Hilton Street and the six on Port Street, for where there is noise there is industry and that of course meant thirsty workers.

I doubt that any of them would recognise the area today because some of the properties dating from the period do still exist like the ones on the opposite side of Port Street, but much of the rest is a haphazard set of buildings plonked down with no coherent plan, but that was pretty much what happened to Mr. Stevenson's grand vision. The fact that St Clements was built a decade after the streets were laid out suggests that all had not gone well.

Indeed, had we walked down Hilton Street, we would have

encountered not only those factories, but also several arms of the Rochdale Canal, which led off the main canal and ran into warehouses on Back China Lane and what is now Tariff Street.

And our walk will now take us from Hilton Street across the car park which was part of the Dale Street Canal Basin, over the Vantage Quay Bridge and by degrees on to Ducie Street and the Jolly Angler.

Jolly Angler...
once the Mather Street School.

Now the Jolly Angler is our destination, but if you were so minded and given kind weather, you could take a walk along the towpath of the Ashton Canal across east Manchester all the way to Ashton. But that is a long very long trek and the alternative might be the short stretch of the Rochdale Canal which runs through the heart of the city and comes out at Castlefield. It is possible to start at Dale Street, but the bit under London Road can

Jolly Angler 1970

be isolated and lonely, so for me it really should be approached from Princess Street. And that short walk should remind us that

the canal network stretched out, offshoots running into warehouses, going underground and linking up with each other across the city.

But that is for a book on the Canals of Manchester so it's back to

Ducie Street and the short stroll down to the Jolly Angler

Now had we done the journey in 1850, it would have taken us along the three streets, because back then Ducie Street stopped at the junction with what is now Jutland Street, continued on its way as Wittles Croft before becoming Mather Street which joined Great Ancoats Streets.

Nor would you have found the Jolly Angler; instead, the site was occupied by the Mather Street School with separate classrooms for boys and girls. And beside the school was the Temperance Hall, which might have been a sore point for the members given that just a little further up Mather Street was the brewery run by Mr. Bottomley and the pub, the Lord Nelson.

The school remains a shadowy place, and despite searching the directories, the references to the place are pretty limited, consisting of two dated 1849 and 1850 from the OS map and Mr. Adshead's remarkable map. It was "independent" and may only have been open on Sundays.

More promising was the Ancoats Lyceum, opened in 1835 as an educational institute, where the "three R's" were taught. It had day schools, evening schools, a newsroom and library, and lectures were occasionally given by prominent men, amongst whom were Mr. Leo Grindon and Mr. T. Wilkinson.

In 1850, the weekly average at the day school was 243, and the number of volumes issued from its library was 4,995.

Its annual tea parties were held in the Mather Street Temperance Hall.

Soon after it opened, one correspondent to the Manchester Guardian wrote that its working was, "in the highest degree satisfactory to its supporters".*

I doubt I will ever get to know if Mr. Bottomley the brewer ever called in at the Lyceum, but he did occupy his brewery for a big chunk of the middle years of the 19th century and may have done so.

That said, I suspect he would have been more than a bit surprised at the changes to the area which continue apace,

and so, while there are still some industrial buildings, the trend is for more of those inner city blocks of flats whose inhabitants would be rewarded with a visit to the Jolly Angler offering them some continuity with the past.

*Lyceum, A Native of Salford, Manchester Guardian November 10, 1838 Salford

Brunswick...

just down from the railway station.

Now it's odd what you remember about a pub. Sometime
around 1971, I was desperately out to impress the parents of
the then love of my life. They were down from the North East
and had booked tickets to see Tony Bennett at the Palace. I
was invited along and, after a meal at a Wimpy on Piccadilly,
with time to spare, we fell into the Brunswick.

I have no memory of what we drank or what the place
looked like, but in the course of researching the pub, one of the
most striking facts is that it has retained that light bright

Brunswick Hotel 1971

exterior. Mostly it was white, but sometimes, as now, it has gone in for a cream colour.

I have no idea how far back that painted exterior goes but I do know that the

pub was serving up beer by 1850.

And just possibly it will have been visited by some of the earnest young clerks who worked round the corner on Dale Street at the offices of the Rochdale Canal Company, which is a good reason for a canal story even if the link is a bit tenuous.

But as my mother always used to say if you want to understand a place you have got to explore it. So, after leaving the Brunswick, walk the few hundred yards to Lena Street, turn left and stroll along this narrow street to Dale Street, opposite which there is a fine stone arch which once gave access to the canal basin.

Now it is a car park, but there are some splendid views of the old warehouse and of course the canal.

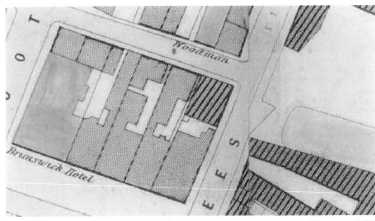

The Brunswick and Lena Street 1851

The Waldorf...

the name which is a mystery.

I really would like to have met Mr. Louis Wahlhauser if only to get his side of the story about the Waldorf on Gore Street.

According to one history, the pub dates from the 1880s when he named it after a Victorian general who was visiting Manchester to open a lodge of the Masons.

Part of my problem is that the source in question spells the pub's name slightly differently to that of the general, and by one of those annoying hiccups in the historical record, the street and trade directories list only the name of the landlord not the name of the pub.

Gore Street William Deacons Bank Waldorf at end 1963

Added to which, by the 1920s the place had become the Waldorf, all of which is most unsatisfactory.

Nor do the maps help because from the 1840s into the 1890s there is no reference to a pub on Gore Street, and, while the Fire Insurance map of 1900 records a public house, it sits there with no name.

Instead, I will go off and explore the life of Mr. Wahlhauser who was born in Germany in 1847, was married in 1870 to the daughter

of a sea captain and, by 1881, was running a boarding house opposite what is now the Waldorf.

Later - much later - it appears to have gone up market, trading as the Temperance Hotel, but later still had reverted to a plain "boarding house", and by 1911 had become a printers.

By then, Mr. Wahlhauser had himself moved on, first to Moss Side and finally to Blackley and during that time his

fortunes seem to have ebbed.

In 1881, he had run the boarding house; a decade later and he described himself as a "hotel porter" and in 1911 a "hotel servant".

Not that he had owned the boarding house.

The rates show that he was merely the tenant running the business and so far his name fails to appear on any other rate record.

Added to which, by 1886 the pub is listed under the name of another landlord.

All of which makes Mr. Wahlhauser a continuing enigma and gets us no further with the name of that pub. Nor, I suspect, just what the inside looked like when he was there.

We had arrived just weeks after a makeover, which had seen the pub get a new coat of paint on the outside and a bit of tender care and attention inside.

It is bright and fresh looking with the usual prints and paintings on the wall and that arresting coloured glass window above the entrance.

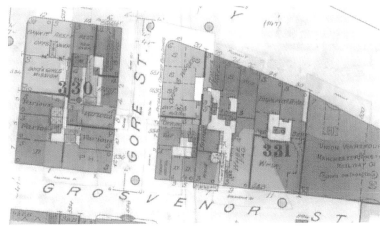

The Waldorf and Grosvenor Street circa 1880

CANAL SIDE
Two railway stations, a canal,
that Fire Station and three more
iconic buildings.

Canal Side

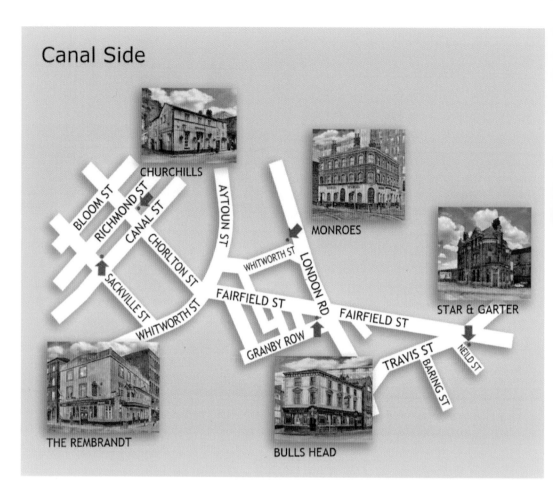

CHURCHILLS

BLOOM ST

RICHMOND ST

CANAL ST

CHORLTON ST

SACKVILLE ST

WHITWORTH ST

AYTOUN ST

WHITWORTH ST

FAIRFIELD ST

GRANBY ROW

LONDON RD

MONROES

FAIRFIELD ST

TRAVIS ST

BARING ST

NEILD ST

STAR & GARTER

THE REMBRANDT

BULLS HEAD

Now in the space of a short walk the curious tourist will be presented with some pretty fine buildings along with the ghosts of many others.

Starting with the ghosts, just on the edge of our walk was the Dolls Hospital which was beside the now vanished Imperial Hotel. Anyone wishing the service of the doll doctor and nurse went up an uninviting staircase into a room with jars of bits and pieces which were used for repairing and making good the damaged but much loved toys.

Nearby was the Coach and Horses which would not have been out of place in a novel by Charles Dickens. You entered by a flight of stone steps and went down a narrow corridor into a small front room and all the beer came in long straight glasses. That said I am prepared to be corrected on that memory given it will be nearly a full half century ago that I was in there.

But I am more confident about the Fire Station which was

opened in 1906, designed by Woodhouse, Willoughby and Langham in red brick and terracotta and costing £142,000 to build.

In addition to the police station, there was a fire station, an ambulance station, a bank, a Coroner's Court, and a gas-meter testing station.

The fire station operated for 80 years, housing the firemen, their families, and the horse drawn appliances that were replaced by motorised vehicles a few years after its opening.

It remained the headquarters of the Manchester Fire Brigade until the brigade was replaced by the Greater Manchester Fire Service in 1974 and it closed in 1986.

London road Fire Station 1940

*The Stranger's Guide to Manchester, H F Duffield

Monroes...

the one that that changed its location.

Now I remember Monroes long before it was Monroes, when it was the White Hart.

And back then, if you walked along that bit of Whitworth Street there was Placemate which had once been the Twisted Wheel and beyond that, roughly where the big blue and while parking sign stands, was Bert's cafe which did a pretty neat sausage sandwich. Between them, you had all you might need for a night out and the morning after, and while the club and cafe have gone, the late reveller can take advantage of the fact that Monroes is also a guesthouse with seven bedrooms.

So, after a night admiring the Marilyn Monroe memorabilia in the bar which stretch to pictures on the ceiling, you can slide

Monroes (White Hart Hotel) 1961

upstairs, comfortable in the knowledge that in the morning there will be a "Full English" on offer.

Over breakfast, the rested guest might ponder on the site of the Old White Hart which once stood in a terrace of properties backing on to a maze of closed courts and back to back houses.

And then in the late 19th century the pub became a corner plot when Whitworth Street was cut, providing it with a more prominent position. All of which offers up the prospect of an adventure after breakfast.

For those interested in the story of live music in the city, the short walk up Whitworth Street to Aytoun Street

239

will take you to Aytoun Street Campus.

This was once the College of Commerce, but which we who spent three years there called the College of Knowledge.

From 1969 to 1973, I rubbed shoulders with students pursuing a mixed bag of subjects from law and business studies to librarianship and the Arts.

But what marked out the college was that it was also the venue for a series of Saturday night gigs with groups as varied as Pink Floyd, the Moody Blues, Barclay James Harvest, Fleetwood Mac, Roy Harper, Canned Heat, and the Edgar Broughton Band.*

I must confess I had forgotten that many of these groups had performed in the hall beside the tower block, but, as they say about so much of the 1960s, "if you can remember it, you weren't there". Looking back at the list and matching the dates, most of the shows happened in the year before I arrived, so perhaps I can be excused.

That said, it would be nice if one of those blue plaques appeared on the wall of the building, although modesty forbids from suggesting that my name along with those of Mike, Lois, John and Jack should be added.

*Setlists FM,
http://www.setlist.fm/venue/college-of-commerce-manchester-england-6bd7a266.html

The Star & Garter...

same name different building and sited a just a short walk from its original location.

The Star and Garter on Fairfield Street is one of those pubs that most people know, even if they have never stepped inside.

It is a magic place, part old fashioned pub, but also a venue for live music and a place which many people will remember with affection.

It has stood on the corner of Travis and Fairfield Street since at least 1879, and moved from its previous site between 1876 and 1879. That previous site was on Boardman Street, which is now Baring Street, and where the pub once stood is at present just a bit of open land on the corner of Fairfield Street.

Looking towards Piccadilly Station, The Star & Garter on the left 1970

Now, depending on which source you read, the original Star and Garter opened in 1801 or 1803, when an enterprising individual saw the potential in an area which was fast being developed with residential, industrial and commercial properties.

That said, the name of the pub doesn't appear in any of the early street directories, although it is clearly labelled on both the 1849 OS map and the Adshead's map of 1851. Of course, its absence from the street directories proves nothing, given that Boardman Street doesn't appear in any listings.

In the meantime, I shall just ponder on the name of Mayfield, which is currently associated with the disused railway station and was once the site of two

schools and nine properties, of which five were back to back, while, a century before, the area was shown as Mayfield. And that raises the tantalizing question of whether the name will survive into the future and, equally, what the fate of the pub might be. The plans for the expansion of Piccadilly railway station will bring two newly constructed platforms very close to the pub, while the owners of Mayfield Station

want to redevelop the area.

The worst case scenario would be that the pub would go, and, if it did, another bit of the musical history of the city would disappear.

There will be many with fond memories of nights spent with their musical heroes, and Andrew, who owns the pub, has created a Facebook page full of photographs of the events that have taken place here.*

And, as it turns out, the Courteeners on their wonderful record "Not Nineteen Forever", mention the place.**

Nor is it just music, because the pub is that sort of place that film makers fall over themselves to use, and so in no particularly order over the last few decades the film credits include: Band of Gold, Cracker, Prime Suspect, There's Only One Jimmy Grimble, Mine All Mine, Prey, The Body Far, Cradle To Grave, Snodgrass, Worried About The Boy, Funland and Dead Clever.

The Star & Garter dancing up stairs 2010

All of which I suspect means that the curious will be off exploring their old box sets to identify the moment when Jane Tennyson in Prime Suspect stands in the almost identical spot inhabited by Dr Edward "Fitz" Fitzgerald from the series Cracker.

At which point, the pedant armed with 54 hours of set box

viewing will set me straight about which characters from these and the other films stood by Andrew's bar.

And as you do, Peter, Andrew and I then got involved in a discussion as to whether the staircase in the pub features in that film, Hell is a City, starring Stanley Baker.

In the end, we decided it didn't, but along the way Andrew pointed out the evidence of a long vanished fireplace, and the tiles in the urinal, all of which helps tell the story of the Star and Garter.

*The Star and Garter, facebook, www.facebook.com/pg/StarAndGarterManchester/photos/?tab=albums
**"Not Nineteen Forever", the Courteeners, www.youtube.com/watch?v=k4Xnou7cq3c

Bulls Head...

the one that saw off its rivals.

Now the Bull has staying power because, despite the redevelopment all around the pub in the late 19th and early 20th centuries, it survived. Less lucky were lots of small properties, several streets, two closed courts and the Wheatsheaf public house. They all went during a realignment of the street pattern and later the construction of the Fire Station.

But the Bull saw them all out. It was there by 1828 and may date back to the 1780s. That said, for some odd reason it was left off the OS map for London Road in 1849 but was back two years later on Adshead's map.

And, like all good survivors, it clung on despite a serious challenge from a rival which was not a pub but The Manchester Coffee Tavern Company Limited, which was a temperance organisation with 15 branches from Piccadilly, down to

Liverpool Road, across to Gaythorn and up to Cannon Street and into Salford.

Its headquarters was the building beside the Bull and the name of The Manchester Coffee Tavern Company Limited is picked out in brick above the entrance.

Coffee was cited by some doctors at the time as a cure for alcoholism and the company made great strides in offering an

The Bulls Head 1963

alternative place for people to meet and relax. The company distributed tokens to the poor, which were only redeemable at their taverns, and this it was hoped would keep working men and women out of licensed premises.

The Manchester Coffee Taverns opened in 1873 and its first eight premises were pulling up to 65,000 visitors per week, even providing separate rooms for young people.

I can't be exactly sure when our building was constructed, but it will have been between 1895 and 1903 when the headquarters of the company were based in

our building at no. 8 Fairfield Street. By 1909, they had vacated the Fairfield Street premises, which became a wholesale milliners, leaving the Bull to continue to offer a different form of refreshment.

And no doubt the pub was popular with some of the passengers who used the nearby London Road Railway Station. It had opened in 1842 as Store Street, changed its name to London Road with a makeover in 1960 when it became Piccadilly Railway Station, before undergoing a second transformation at the beginning of the 21st century when the concourse was redesigned.

For those who like railway stations, there is also the old Mayfield Station, opened in 1910 as an overspill for London Road. It closed to passenger traffic in 1968, was briefly a parcels depot and, since the 1980s, has waited for someone to come up with a new use for the place.

Recently, that new lease of life looked to be a railway station, to relieve the pressure on Piccadilly, but the owners are now looking to redevelop the entire site with a mix of business and residential properties.

All of which might provide new customers for the Bull.

The Bulls Head 1963

Churchills...

from tradesmen to politician.

Churchills was once the Mechanics Arms and you can see how that earlier name fitted well with the area back in the middle 19th century, for here were a mix of industrial enterprises hard by the canal, and, in its way, the pub still reflects its location.

Today, as Churchills, it is one of the Gay pubs in the Village with an interior that is bright and impressive.

The old Mechanics Arms has extended into what was once the cafe on the corner of Chorlton Street and Canal Street.

Churchills (Mechanics Arms) 1959

And here is one of those lessons in always keeping a close eye on how the city is changing. I remember that cafe and will have fallen across its door as a student. It was a modest no nonsense cafe, specialising in strong tea, and fry ups. It didn't pretend to be anything more than a cheap and cheerful eating place.

Opening early, they catered for all those going into work, stayed open for the lunch time trade and pretty much shut up shop in the late afternoon.

But the cafe has gone, as has the old Employment Exchange on Aytoun Street, now replaced by a hotel. The Labour Exchange was designed in 1936 and completed in 1948 after the war and, while some liked its appearance, I have to agree with Pevsner who described it as, "Brick thin and cheap".*

More impressive was the City and Police Sessions Courts on Minishull Street which were built sometime between 1867 and 1872. They are now part of the Crown Courts and underwent a

makeover, including an extension which was finished in 1996.

Churchills (Mechanics Arms) 1973

And while that extension has been sympathetically done, it is the details from the old building which I like best. These include those fierce looking animal carvings at eye level on either side of the entrance, which I suspect were designed to make all who entered reflect on the power of justice and, above all, challenge those harbouring deep and troublesome secrets.

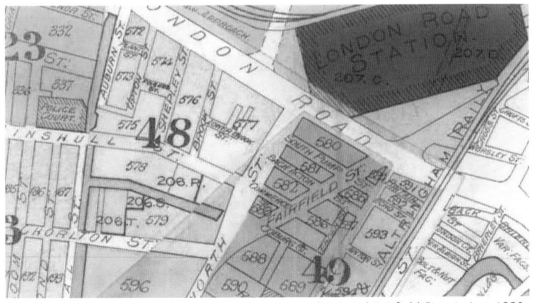

London Road Fairfield Street circa 1880s

*Manchester Clare Hartwell 2001 p145

The Rembrandt...

another with a name change.

The Rembrandt was once the Ogdens Arms and was serving beer on the corner of Sackville Street and Canal Street by 1849, and after a pleasant afternoon in the pub or even before, I think we should conclude with a bit of sightseeing, starting with the old Central School for Boys and Girls on Whitworth Street which is now part of Manchester City College, but in 1914 was taken over as the 2nd Western General Hospital.

Rembrandt Hotel 1971

Almost opposite is the very imposing Sackville Street Building opened in 1902 and the main building for the University of Manchester Science & Technology, while across the road is the Aytoun Building, once the College of Commerce, or, as I referred to it earlier, the College of Knowledge.

All of which just leaves a bit of the Rochdale Canal, a couple of former warehouses and the lock keeper's house on Aytoun Street, along with two railway stations.

Of the two railway stations, only one is left. This is Piccadilly which has had two substantial "makeovers" since it

opened as Store Street in 1842. It later became London Road Railway Station and will soon be expanded by another two platforms.

The other railway station is Mayfield which lasted just half a century, but more of this one later.

The canal has fared better. It was finished in 1804 and ran for 32 miles across the Pennines, of which the last stretch will take you from the Dale Street Basin behind Piccadilly down to the Castlefield Basin. Like all our waterways, it went through

uncertain times, but is now back, fully operational and offering an interesting route through the heart of the city.

Sadly, many of the arms which ran off from the canal to service warehouses, timber yards and mills have gone, although there is the hint of the one that stood between Chorlton Street and Aytoun Street and best seen from Canal Street.

The route of this arm of the canal is now underneath the car park and tower block of the Aytoun Street Building, and explains why the back of the Minto & Turner warehouse and the one next door open out onto nothing more than an open space.

And here for the collector of lost and forgotten streets of Manchester is Little David Street. It is off Chorlton Street, is very narrow and is squeezed between two former warehouses.

A century and half ago, Little David Street was fronted on its east side by a row of fourteen back to back houses and ran parallel with Back Canal Street and both gave access from Chorlton Street to a branch of the Rochdale Canal, which stretched from the main canal almost down to what is now Whitworth Street.

The inhabitants of Little David Street won't feature on any street directory, but they will be on the census returns, along with the landlord of the Mechanics Arms which is now Churchill's, which is as good a link to our pubs as you can get.

CHORLTON ST BUS STATION

Mixing the grand with the mean, the modern with the old and throwing in a dollop of history.

Chorlton St Bus Station

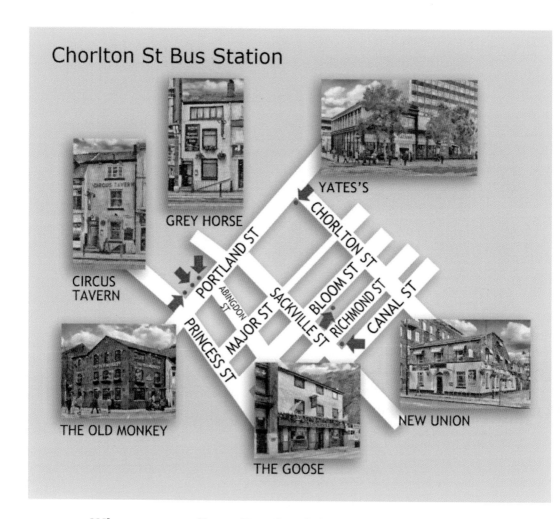

CIRCUS TAVERN

GREY HORSE

YATES'S

PORTLAND ST

CHORLTON ST

ABINGDON ST

MAJOR ST

SACKVILLE ST

BLOOM ST

RICHMOND ST

CANAL ST

PRINCESS ST

THE OLD MONKEY

THE GOOSE

NEW UNION

When you walk up Portland Street, you are never far from that simple observation that the rich and the poor existed cheek by jowl.

So at one end of Portland Street is the Watts Building which is now the Britannia Hotel, but was once the warehouse of S and J Watts, although to call it a warehouse is to short change the building, which was designed to impress the company's customers, along with their rivals and for good measure pretty much everyone else.

It was opened in 1856; each of its five floors represented a different style of Italian architecture and it was the biggest single textile warehouse in the city.

Step out along Chorlton Street which runs beside this fine building and within a few paces to the south down Silver Street, were a warren of small closed courts leading off narrow alleys filled with small back to back houses.

They were not perhaps the worst the city had to offer, but neither were they the best. In his case notes during the cholera outbreak of 1832, Dr. Gautier offers up a vivid picture of the area. Chorlton Street, he wrote, "was tolerably clean and open but the vicinity crowded and populous".

But the home of the Bullock family was dire. Mr. and Mrs. Bullock lived in one room with their two children and Mr. Bullock's mother. The room was on the upper storey of a "filthy and crowded house" and was equally as "filthy". Even before they contracted cholera, none were seen to be in good health and baby Martha aged eight months was "rickety, and emaciated". In the course of just one week they all died of cholera.*

A month later, Dr. Gautier was back in Silver Street attending Jane White who lived in a cellar and who died just days after contracting the disease.

Today, Chorlton Street and Silver Street look far removed from the mass of courts, alleys and crowded houses of 1832, and that stretch of Silver Street occupied by Jane White is now underneath Chorlton Street Bus Station.

It was opened in 1950, redesigned in 1967 with the addition of the multi-story car park and had a major rebuild in 2002.

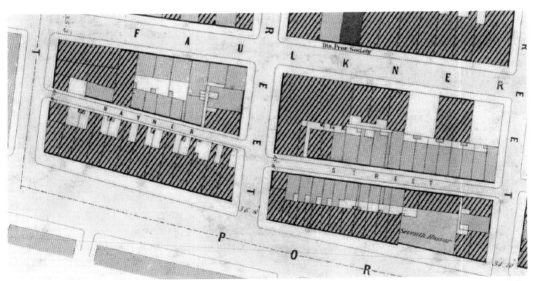

Portland Street 1851

*The Origin and Progress of the Malignant Cholera in Manchester, Henry Gautier M.D., 1833 case notes no. 5-8, page 162 and no. 71, page 178

Yates's...

in a tradition stepping back into the middle of the 19th century.

The Yates's on Portland Street isn't old although it is part of Britain's first chain of pubs and stands on the site of a bank and later one of those all-purpose Manchester buildings which managed to cram a number of different businesses inside its walls.

For those of a certain age, a Yates' will always be linked to a pretty basic drinking place with bare floor boards, simple decor and, above all, the Blob, made from sweet Australian wine and brandy, sugar, lemon and hot water.

And it was the one place I could be certain of buying a bottle of white port which was the favourite tipple of my friend Ann who had a shed load of stories of nights out in a Yates's.

All of which is in direct contrast with the one on the corner of Portland and Chorlton Street. It is a large spacious place

Before Yates's wine lodge 1866

which was already full at midday when we called in. They were a mix of German football fans, marking time before they made their way across town, a few couples having a bite to eat and a bunch of tourists.

The area that surrounds it has also been through more than a few changes, with tall office blocks replacing a mix of Victorian and Edwardian buildings, some less

distinguished than others and some less missed than others. One that many regret being demolished was York House on

Major Street. It only dated from 1911 and went in 1974, but was one of those remarkable buildings that caught your eye and always delighted me.

I always thought it had been a design studio because the rear was entirely glazed with each of the seven storeys stepped back from the lower one and each floor consisting of vertical lean-to glazing running the width of the floor to maximise the amount of light entering the building.

Years later, I discovered that it was nothing more grand than a packing warehouse and as such the planners were not interested in it, so despite a planning enquiry, it was knocked down as part of a plan to build a new road system, with a proposed office block on the site of York House.

The road was never built and in 2016 the site of this iconic lost building is still a car park, but it isn't all gloom, for just around the corner at 103 Princess Street is the imposing Mechanics Institute where the Trades Union Congress first met in 1868.

Grey Horse Inn...

selling beer with Mr. and Mrs. Rustrick from 1851.

The Grey Horse is one of those pubs which seems to have history coming out of its walls.

It didn't start as a pub. In 1850, it was occupied by Frank Rustrick who lived with his wife Martha and a lodger. In the December of 1850, he had described himself as a "maker up" but by the April

Grey Horse Inn 1971

of the following year was selling beer.*

I suppose he just saw the sense of switching trades and, in 1851, of the eleven houses running from Nicholas Street to Princess Street five were beer shops.

They will have all been much the same with the front room serving the beer and the back room and upper floors given over to living quarters.

And walking into the Grey Horse will be pretty much how a typical beer shop would have been back

in the 1850s, although now the back room is an extension of the pub. The long windows on the top floor do suggest that it was once used for handloom weaving and a walk along Reyner Street which runs directly behind will reveal that a number of the properties have those same tell-tale long windows.

But before you step out into the street and leave the ghost of the Rustrick's behind, you might ponder that under your feet in 1851 lived the Bury family who occupied the cellar. Mr.

James was a "boot and shoe maker" and he and his wife Mary lived with their four children in the room below you.

The staircase down to that cellar is still there, but the curious pub goer might be more interested in the building next door at number 82 Portland

Street which is odd.

It stands between the row of late 18th century houses, but is clearly not one of them, so while the surrounding properties are typical of the type being built across the city, many of which included workshops on the upper floor, number 82 is different.

In 1851, it was home to William McCann and his mother Elizabeth. William was a painter and perhaps was doing alright because they occupied the place on their own, but their home was demolished in 1883 and our tall intruder took its place. It was to become the offices of the Great Eastern Railway Company and was still dealing in orders and answering enquiries in 1911.

All of which just leaves me to reflect on the more recent passage of time, because, in the time Peter painted the Grey Horse, it has had a makeover.

Gone are those yellowing cream walls and the wrought iron work at the windows, and in their place a smart white exterior and a new sign.

*Census for Portland Street Enu1x 9-11 Market Street Manchester1851

Circus Tavern...
memories of a lock in.

Now the Circus is a pub I have very fond memories of. Once, back in the 1980s on a Saturday night, we wandered in around 9 in the evening. There were three other customers and just an hour or so later, as we were into a third round, the landlord locked the front door.

Circus Tavern 1957

I guess he had worked out he would make enough to cover the night's takings and didn't have to bother about drunken punters falling in just before closing time.

I have no idea if this was a common practice but the idea of a lock in, even if it was still while the pub was officially open appealed to all of us.

Walking into the place recently, it didn't seem to have changed over much in three decades. The small bar faces you and the two rooms are off the narrow corridor. Back in 1850, it seems that its occupant was one of the many in the city who sold beer as a side line, for while Mr. Clarkson listed himself as "a beer retailer", the following year he described himself as an "engine fitter". Now there is nothing surprising in what seems

to be a dual occupation. People often set up as beer sellers to tide themselves over a short period of unemployment or as a secondary income.

Of the three pubs still

271

remaining on the row, it is the oldest, although back in 1850 its then landlord, a Mr. Henry Clarkson, faced competition from Frank Rustick at number 80 Portland and Alice Ormer at 88, and the Three Legs of Man Tavern run by Mary George at number 90.*

It remains a very popular pub and, on the day we were there, a group of six from Bolton were happily on their third round having originally planned to do some sight-seeing and early Christmas shopping. Needless to say, it looked as if neither objective would be accomplished and the best one of them had to offer up was a postcard of the Town Hall.

But they were more than happy to have their photograph taken. As one said "it isn't every day that you get to leave Bolton for the day and get your picture taken".

Not that everyone in the pub on that day was so keen to have their fifteen minutes of fame. One chap at the bar declined Peter's offer, commenting that he would rather not let his employers know where he went in the dinner hour.

In the interests of sound research, we were back the following day at the same time but neither the Bolton band nor the reluctant office worker were to be seen.

In their place were two Japanese tourists and a postman from New Zealand, and, as much as I was tempted, I didn't ask the postman if he had a special delivery for the staff or if he planned to be back in Wellington for closing time.

Circus Tavern 1970

*Census for Portland Street Enu1x 9-11 Market Street Manchester1851

The Old Monkey...
new but with a hint of continuity.

Despite its name, the Old Monkey is a new pub. It was opened in 1993 but can claim to stand on a site which was "doing beer" by the middle of the 19th century. In 1850 Kitty Fletcher was listed as a beer retailer, and shared the premises with Bonsall and Rushton estate agents and the Three Legs of Man Tavern run by Mary George.

That remains a bit of a mystery, made even muddier by the fact that the following year all three had gone, in favour of a cooper and his family and a locksmith who lived in the cellar, but the property continued to be listed as selling beer.

All of which will mean little to those who have wandered into the Old Monkey, but at least they may have a sense of continuity as they order their beer and look at the food menu,

Old Monkey (Queens Arms) 1904

with the added superiority of knowing that the building was briefly also home to the Portland Bookshop after the Queen's Hotel stopped serving.

Something of the name also lasted well into the 1970s, because part of what is now the Monkey was the Queens Cafe,

a place I visited on many occasions back in the day.

And that leaves one last building, or more accurately one cellar, which was the Conti Club on Harter Street. Some will insist on calling it the New Conti which indeed it was because the old Conti on Oxford

Road had closed in the mid 1960's, and its owners shifted location to Harter Street where it remained, offering late night booze, questionable food and a happy bunch of people until it closed in 2001.

Strictly speaking, the Conti was the Continental Club. It was much favoured by doctors and nurses, and, while we never crossed paths, both my old friend Sally, who was a nurse, and I remember it very fondly. It was a place you either took to or

loathed. Another friend once described it as "a bus shelter with booze" which was a tad unfair and missed the point that this was one of those happy places where you went after the pub, usually in groups but sometimes on your

Watercolour by Evacustes A. Phipson 1925

own looking for a friend.

It was a place where all things were possible, including the night fifteen rugby players from Liverpool stripped naked and conga danced out of the club and into the night.

I make no apologies about including the Conti; it was after all a feature of the city's nightlife for decades. It would be nice to think that someone might put a plaque on its wall. It was briefly the subject of a Facebook site calling for its return, but in 2015 plans were submitted for the conversion of the entire building into 22 one and two bed apartments, and the finished properties are on the market now.*

Maybe the developers will put up a plaque commemorating many happy and more than a few drunken nights in memory of the New Conti, 1967-2001.

*2 Harter Street, 105885/FO/2014/C2, Manchester City Council Planning portal

The Goose...

another pub with almost as many names as the number of coaches departing from the bus station opposite.

Some will remember the pub as Paddy's Goose and according to one source, it also traded variously as the Rams Head and the Kingston, but for most of its existence it was the Fleece Tavern and as such served the occupants of the large numbers of terraced houses that surrounded it during the mid - 19th century.

And like pubs everywhere it survived the house clearances, to find a whole new set of customers who worked in the warehouses which replaced the rows of workers homes. These were supplemented from 1950 by those passing through the coach station directly opposite.

Although I have to say that, in those days before coaches were fitted with

The Goose (The Kingston) 1970

lavatories, those who indulged in a long lingering set of pints before finally embarking on an equally long, slow and torturous journey were far braver than I.

But judging by the customers that we both encountered on our last visit that seemed less of a problem.

More than a few were locals who had chosen city centre living over suburbia and for them a fourth pint presented no great challenge at all. Instead they looked to an afternoon of uninterrupted conversations and good beer. Not even the distraught man from Leeds who had lost his bus ticket seemed to cause them a stir.

Now while we are on names, this may be the moment to share the mystery of the pub which couldn't decide how many Hussars it had served.

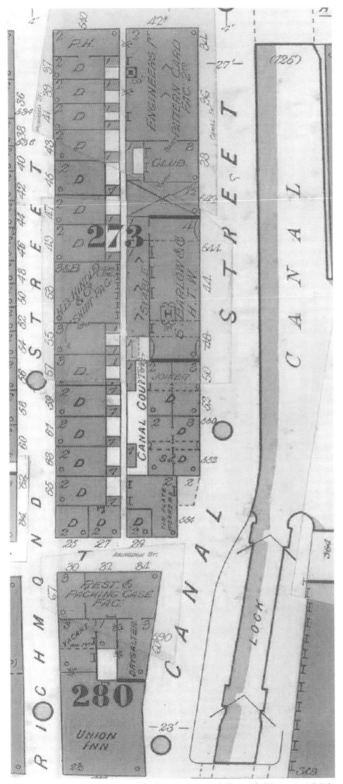

Union Inn and Canal Street 1880s

It stood on Portland Street close to Charlotte Street and in 1828 was the 15th Hussars, but by 1851 strangely it was down to the 7th Hussars having temporarily become just the Hussar Tavern in 1850, before quickly vanishing a decade later.

This is the sort of silly bit of information for a pub quiz and is well worth storing up with that equally fascinating piece of information that the pub round the corner was for most of its time just called the Union but after a refurbishment the owners added "New" to the title in the 1970s.

The New Union...

at the heart of the community.

   The New Union stands on the corner of Princess Street and
Canal Street in The Village and was one of the first gay
establishments in the city. The building, according to some
sources, was built in 1865, but there was already a pub here
trading as the Union in 1850. Back then, it competed with the
Ogden Arms further up Canal Street, and the Mechanics Arms.

   That said, with the Rochdale Canal directly opposite, and
plenty of warehouses and coal yards as well as a textile mill and
machine works close by, I suspect it will have had plenty of
customers. By the end of the century it had seen off its rival
and is now part of the very popular area known as The Village.

Union Hotel 1970

The surrounding area suffered a bit during the second half of the last century.

I remember the streets around the New Union were gloomy and uninviting, seen at their worst on a wet Sunday evening with the light fading fast. The office workers would not make an appearance for another few hours, the warehouses were closed and few people lived in the city centre. The best fun that you might offer a visitor was to count the parking meters on Canal Street and watch the

collection of discarded plastic bottles floating on the water of the canal.

Even regular Saturday student events at the old College of Knowledge failed to lift the gloom.

If memory serves me

correctly, Canned Heat played there, although like so much of my Saturday nights in the late 1960s and 70s, the consumption of much Newky Brown dimmed the reality. I can't say that Newcastle Brown Ale was that appealing but it came in bottles and so had the advantage over a pint glass on the dance floor.

And if all that is now a challenge to what I can remember, so is the story of the night thieves who stole the takings from the Student's Union bar after a very successful night and dumped the safe in the canal.

So the opening of Manto in 1990 marked the beginnings of the transformation of the area

from sad and empty into a vibrant centre. The gay pubs were now joined by a host of bars and restaurants, there was an openly supportive position from Manchester City Council and today, on any night of the week, including Sundays, the area is alive.

All of which may seem a long way away from when the residents of the surrounding streets made the Union their local, but I think not. Just like then, the Village is a community and if not all of the people who inhabit the bars and restaurants live there, it is a place which lots of people identify with and have a fondness for and that for me is a community.

OXFORD RD
Crossing the River Medlock and
the Rochdale Canal.

Oxford Rd

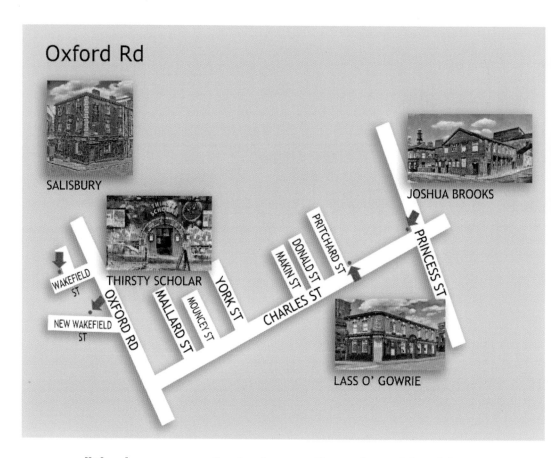

"the huge manufacturies .... the miserable chimney tops of Little Ireland, down by the dirty Medlock .... dingy streets, swarming with dingy people"*

As a description of the streets off Oxford Street in 1857 Mr. Muir's comments may seem a bit over the top, but it was what he saw, staring down from the vantage point of a railway viaduct on his way to the pleasant and open countryside of Chorlton and Stretford.

Had he done that journey just 70 years earlier, he might well have left the main road and sat in any one of a number of fields along the southern banks of the River Medlock and composed a piece on the delights of the area, commenting on the number of ponds and clumps of trees, speculating on how soon the area would be developed by those wanting to escape Manchester.

Nor would he have had long to wait; by the mid - 1790s, maps show that the main streets we know today were being laid out with fine sounding names, and already businessmen were making use of the water from the river for a whole range of industrial enterprises. All of which meant that in the space of just 40 years those pleasant fields had been lost to textile mills and rows of terraced housing.

And these mills were a tourist attraction. They would have come out of Manchester into Chorlton-upon-Medlock and visited these textile factories which for many were the marvel of the age.

Of course, visiting one and working in one were two very different experiences. Cotton workers suffered from the dust, the noise and the long hours of labour and may not have shared the enthusiasm of the curious visitors, social commentators and novelists who later would reflect on the power, energy and enterprise of what they saw.

Today, after decades of neglect, some of the mills have been converted into apartments for those wanting to live close to the city centre, and in their way have become tourist attractions and vie with a few neighbouring iconic buildings, which include the railway station with its 1960 armadillo roof, the majestic Refuge Building and the Palace Theatre.

The theatre opened in 1891 as the Manchester Palace of Varieties with a spectacular ballet production of Cleopatra followed by a variety show and has pretty much continued to do the business for the last 125 years.

And for those that want to add to their local quiz knowledge, the Palace, the Refuge Building and the Oxford Road railway station are all bound together in the film, 'Hell is a City'.

It was made in 1960 and was shot on location across Manchester and, in one memorable scene, Stanley Baker confronts a criminal on the roof tops of the Refuge Building, against a backdrop of the Palace and the railway station.

Gone now are Gaskell's Baths which included a heated pool and sauna, which one journalist wrote, "sweeps the filth of Manchester out of one's pores" and this was combined with treatments for obesity, rheumatism and sciatica.

They operated from the 1930s through to the 1950s and were located in Imperial Buildings, that large stone building which runs down from the bridge on Oxford Road to Charles Street.

* Lancashire Sketches, Muir, Edwin, 1869, pages 74 & 75

Joshua Brooks...

almost named after a real person.

The Joshua Brooks may look the part, but it is a relatively new pub; even so, according to one source, it was briefly Sofa Central, before returning to its original name, which is apt given that Joshua Brookes was educated at Manchester Grammar School, and from 1790 until his death in 1821 was chaplain at the Collegiate church.

One history of Manchester says he was, "supposed to have baptised, married and buried more persons than any other clergyman in the kingdom. He was a man of great eccentricity, with many failings, but few if any vices. He had a good acquaintance with books and left a good library behind him".*

Mr. Brookes also featured in the book 'The Manchester Man' by Mrs. Linnaeus Banks published in 1876, which everyone claims to have read but which has defeated me twice.

Set in Manchester in the 19th century and following the life of Jabez Clegg's rise to prosperity, it touches on some real

Joshua Brooks (Smith & Dunn Ltd) 1960

historical events including Peterloo, along with some romantic episodes and, if I had persevered, I might have come across a reference to Charles Street, and the site which is now occupied by the pub.

In the 1840s it was a cotton mill, by the late 1890s a bleaching and finishing works, in 1911 a printers and in 1969 was still offering up printed note paper and trade cards.

Alas, I cannot make a link between the pub and either Jabez Clegg or the eccentric Mr. Brookes, although it is worth pointing out that the name of the pub and the man are spelt differently,

so perhaps we need to go looking for another Joshua Brooks.

It is the sort of quest that might just fill an empty few minutes while waiting to be served.

On the other hand, there is always the story of the BBC building which occupied the large site almost

opposite. It stretched from Charles Street down to Brancaster Road and displaced fourteen streets and countless houses.

Planning permission had been granted in 1968 and, after a hiccup, building began in 1971; it was finished in 1975 and the place was home to the BBC until 2011.

And for those wanting to impress a companion, about 800 staff worked there and with the opening of the second studio in 1981 the BBC closed Broadcasting House in Piccadilly which had been there for 52 years.

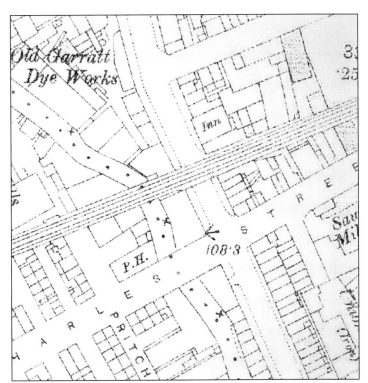

Charles Street Princess Street 1894

*The Annals of Manchester William Axon, editor, 1885, page 164

Lass O'Gowrie...

an odd name.

There is a lot of tosh written about the Lass O'Gowrie which is on Charles Street hard by the Medlock. One of the most common mistakes is that it was in Little Ireland that notorious slum much written about by Dr Kay, Frederick Engels and others.

I suppose it adds something to the pub's profile, but sadly it is just not so. Little Ireland was on the other side of Oxford Street in the bend of the river Medlock and some of it was swept away when the Manchester South and Altrincham Railway was built. What was left pretty much vanished under

Lass O' Gowrie 1959

new textile factories, although two of the streets still existed as entrances to mills on Great Marlborough Street and are still there today.

Of course some of the residents of Little Ireland could have walked the short distance and drank in the Lass O'Gowrie, which was certainly there by 1849 and may have been serving beer on the spot in 1841.

The pub is marked on the 1849 OS map as the Lass O'Gowrie, and eight years earlier it was known as the George IV, which might push back the date when the site was licensed to sometime between 1820 when he came to

the throne and 1830 when he died.

Not that this helps shed any light on the origin of the name

Lass O'Gowrie and so it may well be that, as many have already written, it is in some way connected to the poem the Lass O'Gowrie by the Scottish poet Lady Carolina Nairne.

And that just allows the curious visitor to get distracted by the decor which includes the wood panelling, the bare brick walls and those green tiles.

For those fascinated by the more basic aspects of life there is also that blue sign on the outside of the building but that I will leave you to explore.

And just across the road history is repeating itself with a new development. Once it was home to fourteen streets and countless houses which were all swept away so that the BBC could have a new broadcasting centre here in Manchester.

The lost streets included Pritchard Street, Hesketh, Leigh and Saville Streets and along with the houses there had been a school and a pub. And now in the fullness of time, there will be residents again on the site who no doubt will walk across to the Lass O'Gowrie.

*The Annals of Manchester William Axon, editor, 1885, page 164

The Thirsty Scholar...
the one under the arches.

You would think that a pub underneath a railway line specializing in live music would have a bit of a problem, particularly when the railway line in question carries all the through traffic from north Wales and the North West coast in and out of Manchester. Add to this those long freight trains which seem to go on forever as they slowly shamble through the station and you wonder how the audience can make out the sound of BB King, the best of Motown and selections of Northern Soul.

But it must all work because the pub under the arches next to Oxford Road Railway Station has been going for some time.

Thirsty Scholar 1959

Of course, there will always be those commuters, heading home who after a punishing journey want to start the evening with a drink and if, like me, you tend to end up at a railway station four hours before the train is due, a pint is guaranteed to make the time pass.

It is also a superb meeting up point for one of those walks around the Little Ireland area, a regular feature of the Victorian guided walks and talks.

So having fortified yourself for the

horrors of some dark social history to come, it is a short walk down New Wakefield Street to Great Marlborough Street, taking in the oddly named Frank Street and William Street before deciding that a tour of some of the warehouse and

mill conversions also has a lot going for it.

The story of this area, which was known as Little Ireland, was documented in great detail by both Dr Kay in the 1830s and Frederick Engels a decade later, and is easily accessible.

Suffice to say the description of the roof tops which were visible from Oxford Road are enough to convey the idea that this was not the most pleasant of places to live. The hollow

dropped down from the main road and nestled beside the river which was prone to flooding with unpleasant consequences for those living in the properties.

But despite some attempts by the Corporation to tackle this most awful of awful slums, it was industry which did for the mean houses. Just as at Angel Meadows, some of the worst properties were swept away by new building projects.

And today you will have to

have a particularly good imagination to think yourself back to that time. Not that I think those who occupy the converted factories and the new build would themselves give a second's thought to the misery and squalor which was the lot of those who lived here over 170 years ago.

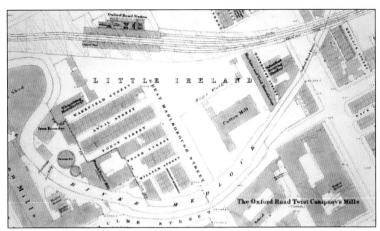

Little Ireland 1849

Today, a stroll down New Wakefield Street, along Great Marlborough Street and then back up Hulme Street is a reminder of how the city is continuing to redevelop.

A visitor who last walked these streets just a decade and a bit ago will be astonished at the changes as the conversions and new build continue apace, all of which makes Dr Kay's and Mr. Engel's descriptions even harder to place.

The Salisbury....

so good they named it twice.

Now the Salisbury on Wakefield Street is another one of those old Manchester pubs which seems to offer the past up with your pint.

Mr. Benjamin Smith was running the place in 1841 and the following year paid an annual rent of £80 to the owner, a Mr. James Whalley, along with a further £66 in rates. However, the original site could be much older and may have already been there by 1819. Thirty years later, it was surrounded by small, mean houses which were packed together in between Oxford

Street and the railway line.

In total, there were three of these narrow streets consisting of James Leigh Street, Cayley Street and Mary Street, which took in 28 small back to back properties.

I can be fairly certain that the three roads post-date 1819 and were there by 1849, but

Salisbury 1959

even so, that 30 years yields up a fair few property owners called Leigh, so it will be a tedious process of elimination.

And on the corner was our pub which was then called the Tulloghgorum Tavern, a name it retained till 1895 when it became the Salisbury.

The origin of its name is obscure but there is a Scottish poem and Highland reel with the same name, and I am reliably informed that in Gaelic the word is variously spelled - Tullochgorm, Tulloch Gorm, Tulloch Gorum, Tulach Gorm. Tulach or Tulloch means a hill, hillock, knoll while Gorm is Gaelic for blue, green, or blue-green, so the meaning of the two words could be translated "blue-green hills".

That said, the change of name is certainly linked to the Conservative leader Lord Salisbury who formed a government in 1895. By then, most of the

mean little streets had gone, cleared away by the railway company, and industry, but it is still possible to get a sense of what it might have been like a century and a half ago.

You drop down from Oxford Street into a hollow and then as now the place is dominated by the tall railway viaduct and two of those narrow streets.

And while the back to backs have long gone, and Little Ireland is just a page in a history book, at least the names of the people who built the houses are still there.

James Leigh, and perhaps his wife or daughter Mary left their mark as did Mr. William and Mr. Frank just round the corner in the streets they built.

We began with Edwin Muir and it is perhaps fitting

we should end where we began, because dominating the area around our four pubs is that railway viaduct which gave him such a lofty position.

He had decided in the winter of 1857 to travel from the heart of the city by train along a railway which was just eight years old. It was a journey of contrasts. Leaving, *"the huge manufacturies, and the miserable chimney tops of Little Ireland, down by the dirty Medlock; we ran over a web of dingy streets, swarming with dingy people.... left the black stagnant canal, coiled in the hollow, stretching its dark length into the distance , like some slimy snake"*. Then, clearing the, *"cotton mills, and dye works, and chemical manufactories of Cornbrook"* , he headed out to the open countryside.*

Few people at that time were afforded the opportunity to look down on their fellow citizens and be able to draw such a lofty and critical judgement. The railway had made that possible and in the course of its building had swept away some of the worst of the housing by the river and Oxford Road, and in the next few years the same relentless drive for re-development may also threaten the Salisbury which, while it escaped the building of the viaduct, may not be so lucky a second time.

* Lancashire Sketches, Muir, Edwin, 1869, pages 74 & 75

PETERSFIELD

Lots of water, two railway stations
and the story of Edna and her
lost underwear.

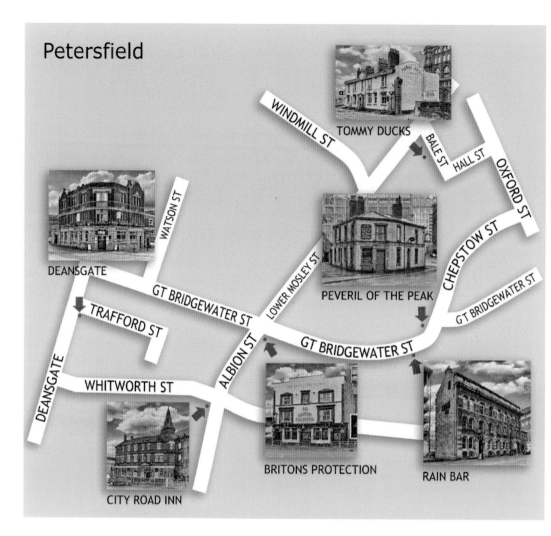

Petersfield

WINDMILL ST

TOMMY DUCKS

BALE ST

HALL ST

OXFORD ST

WATSON ST

CHEPSTOW ST

DEANSGATE

GT BRIDGEWATER ST

GT BRIDGEWATER ST

LOWER MOSLEY ST

PEVERIL OF THE PEAK

TRAFFORD ST

ALBION ST

GT BRIDGEWATER ST

GT BRIDGEWATER ST

DEANSGATE

WHITWORTH ST

BRITONS PROTECTION

RAIN BAR

CITY ROAD INN

Now the route that will take you from Tommy Ducks via Peveril of the Peak, the Rain Bar and Britons Protection down to the City Road Inn and the Deansgate is pretty straightforward and offers up a selection of some of our best buildings.

It starts with the old Central Railway Station with its huge glass and iron roof which remains an impressive sight and faces the equally impressive Midland Hotel.

The station closed just short of its hundredth birthday, was briefly a car park and is now the exhibition centre.

Almost opposite Central is the new Bridgewater Concert Hall which incorporated in its grounds an arm of the Rochdale Canal, which is a reminder that once the canal branched off around the area supplying the needs of the local warehouses and workshops and also connected up with the Manchester and Salford Junction Canal which is the one that ran underground for a stretch.

During the last world war, part of Manchester and Salford was an air raid shelter and it remains a draw for those who like their history in the form of tunnels and hidden passageways.

Alternatively, for those who never lost their fascination for trains and railway stations, there is Knott Mill which now goes under the name of Deansgate, but still carries its original title high up near the roof line.

It has a modest entrance with some ornate ironwork which opens up to the tiled booking hall and the stone steps that lead up to the platforms, and by degrees the foot bridge to the Castlefield - Deansgate metro stop, which commands some of the finest views across this part of the city.

And if by then you are in need of a drink, there are the bars of Deansgate Lock which have been constructed in the arches of the railway viaduct beside the Rochdale Canal on Whitworth Street West.

On a warm summer's evening, sitting on the platform over the water at the Locks has to be one of those special things to do, but I hear you say, "none of these are pubs" so I shall leave them behind and start with the sorry tale of Tommy Ducks on East Street.

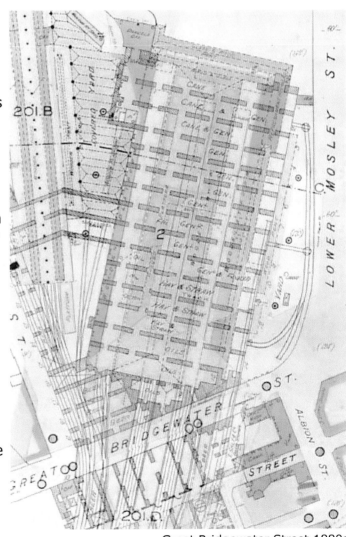

Great Bridgewater Street 1880s

Tommy Ducks ...

underwear, a coffin and a dark deed .... the pub that is no more.

Tommy Ducks still holds a powerful affection for many people and there will be those like Edna who will tell you of the night she donated an item of her underwear which was displayed on the ceiling of the pub beside countless others.

Not that you will find it today because it went one night when no one was looking and its demolition is a story I have to retell to my sisters every time they are up from London.

I first took them there around 1977 and it always ranked alongside the Town Hall, Central Ref and John Rylands as a place to revisit, but so the story goes, the pub's preservation order ran out one Sunday at midnight and couldn't be renewed

Tommy Ducks 1977

till the following morning and in that gap in time a demolition team did the deed.

Less well known perhaps is the skeleton and coffin at Tommy Ducks which I always remember as being in the bay window of the Nags Head in the early 1970s.

What I hadn't known was that, when Ken Riggs who was the landlord of Tommy's moved over to the Nag's Head on Jackson's Row, he took the wooden box complete with bones with him.

And not to be outdone, the new man behind the bar told the Manchester Evening News that, "customers missed the coffin so I called in a firm of masons and they made a headstone in his memory".*

I doubt I would ever have come across the story had it not been for my friend Elaine who worked there and

Tommy Ducks interior and theatre posters 1960

Tommy Ducks Bar 1960

supplied the press cutting which included a photograph of her and Philip Ormrod, the new landlord, beside the headstone.

For some, Elaine will also be remembered as the other half in a tag which appeared across parts of South Manchester in the early 1970s, simply announcing Dennis & Elaine. For a few short years they seemed to be everywhere and then they vanished. Only decades later after writing about the mysterious

Tommy Ducks interior 1960

Dennis and Elaine did I discover her identity and the rest, as they say, is history and a friendship.

But back to Tommy Ducks which dates back into the 19th century and originally occupied just one property at number 8 East

Street, but later extended into the adjacent properties.

There are some photographs of both the exterior and the interior of the pub but what I like about Peter's painting is the detail of a neighbouring building.

And like all good images it draws you in and makes you ask questions.

Look carefully

PHILIP ORMROD, a 27-year-old bachelor, drinks a macabre toast here with barmaid Elaine Church, at the Manchester centre pub of Tommy Ducks, where he has just taken over as licensee.

When previous host Ken Riggs left Tommy Ducks he took with him a coffin and skeleton, a feature at the pub.

Explained Phil: "Customers admired the coffin, so I called in a firm of masons and they made a headstone in his memory. But the skeleton can't rest in peace, actually, because it is now propped up behind a bar at the Nag's Head, Manchester, where Ken went."

Elaine and Philip Ormrod

and still standing beside the end of the pub is a bit of the stone work from the old warehouse next door. This bit of stone formed part of the archway into the inside of the building.

When I first ventured down East Street sometime around 1971, the warehouse was still there, a large gloomy place which passed from one occupant to another.

In 1903, it was the place of work of Edward Samson Bros, merchants, and by 1911 had changed hands and no doubt continued to do so until its final demise.

Back in the 1950s Alan McCarthy remembers both the pub and the surrounding properties.

"In the mid - fifties I was employed with a textile firm just around the corner from East Street where Tommy Ducks was. I remember the ladies knickers and I believe that stars appearing at the Manchester Palace often called in at the pub.

"On East Street there were two cafes who served breakfast for the factory works.

"Also on East Street there was an entry and a man sat there with a table taking bets. One man who worked at our firm was a bookies runner, and one day another man working at the firm won a six horse accumulator and collected £1000 which paid for a holiday to Blackpool".

*The skeleton in the coffin, Manchester Evening News, 1971

Peveril of the Peak...

tiles, history, more than a few celebrities and a football table.

The Peveril of the Peak is one of those gems that is easy to miss, but is a fascinating place.

Inside, it is still divided into small rooms, many retaining the old bell pushes, tiles and other original features. Now I say original features, but I suspect most are late 19th century, while the pub was certainly serving beer as the Peveril of the Peak in 1841, when the landlady was an Elizabeth Johnson.

I would like to know more of Mrs. Johnson but the records are not very helpful. There were a lot of Elizabeth Johnsons in Manchester in 1841 but our candidate may have been a 45 year old widow living with her three sons and a servant.

She is down as running the pub in the January of '41 but seems to have moved on by the June, and a decade later the place is run by someone else.

As for the magnificent exterior tiles, these were added sometime at the beginning of the 20th century by the

Manchester Brewery Company, which did the same to the Sawyers Arms on Deansgate and the Lower Turks Head.

And those tiles are everywhere, including the staircase up to the living quarters and are matched by some more recent ones in the lavatory from Wilson's brewery.

Peveril of the Peak 1896

There are also a shed load of old photographs of the pub including one before it acquired its exterior tiling, and, for those who like spotting celebrities, I will leave you to find the ones of Robbie Coltrane and Bill Bryson, after which there is

always the table football machine which still uses 50 pence pieces.

All of which makes it a very traditional pub and more so because, when Joe and I strolled in one afternoon a few years ago the landlady called time at 3 o'clock.

Now for those who don't know or have forgotten, there was a time when pubs closed in the afternoon and for a few short hours from 3 till 5.30 not a pint was pulled or a gin and tonic

served. It had been a war time regulation introduced during the Great War and had never gone away until 1988 when the restrictions were relaxed and pubs could, if they so chose, stay open from 11 till 11.

But in the Peveril on that day the bell was rung and we were out. I was told recently that it doesn't happen anymore and may even have been a one off. I hope not. I do like tradition.

Rain Bar...

whose name was inspired by an umbrella factory but so easily could have been called Mr. Worthington's or the Foundry.

The Rain Bar is a modern pub. It was opened in 1999 and takes its name from the fact that at one time there was an umbrella factory on the site, but having said that, the brewery could have chosen a name from any one of a number of previous uses for the place.

There was a printing business here along with various manufacturing works, and back in the middle of the 19th century an iron foundry, all of which had access to the canal, which is directly behind the building and today acts as a backdrop for those wanting to sit in the garden, part of which was once Thomas Worthington's Smallwares Cotton Mill.

And those with an interest in canals will want to know that this is the final section of the Rochdale Canal which runs from Piccadilly to Castlefield. Most of it can be walked and it remains a fine way of seeing bits of the city

Rain Bar (once an umbrella factory) 1964

which are otherwise hidden.

Sadly, in the space of the last few decades some of that has gone, including the hospital which for a while was a car park and now is a supermarket and the old pipes which ran from the power station delivering steam to the nearby buildings.

Well into the 1980s they continued to do the business and I was never quite sure if I should feel concerned as wisps of steam came out from the pipe joints.

I suppose my favourite stretch is just past the Rain Bar where the canal goes under Albion Street and you are

presented with a set of lock gates and a tunnel as well as the lock keeper's house.

But we have strayed from the Rain Bar, so I will just mention the little hut for the ducks which sits on that arm of the Rochdale leading to the pub and leave you with another quiz answer which is that once there were a

number of short stretches of the canal that branched off, but this one is the last survivor. It continues on to finish beside the

Bridgewater Concert Hall.

For those who tire of the gardens, the interior of the Rain Bar is very impressive. The pub is on three levels with the upper floors given over to two function rooms and the ground floor split into smaller areas. As befits its workaday origins, there is plenty of exposed brick which may or may not have been part of building, some fine looking beams and that sweeping staircase.

Rain Bar (Stationer & Printer) 1896

The Britons Protection...

continuing to serve the changing population of Great Bridgewater Street.

Now a night in the Britons Protection should bring up more than a few ghosts if you have an imagination.

For me it will be Parker Horsfield who was selling beer and offering up conversation to his customers in 1822. Back then, Great Bridgewater Street was still a developers' paradise and, while there were some properties already surrounding the pub, there was still plenty of open land.

The arrival of the Rochdale Canal at the beginning of the 19th century had fed the development and, by the late 1840s, there was a mix of textile mills, foundries and smaller business accompanied by rows of terraced housing.

All of which will have pleased our Mr. Horsfield and even more his successor, Mr. Jonathan Stanley who had seen the rateable value of the pub increase from £45 in 1822 to £70 by 1851.

Britons Protection 1959

And as these things happen, the building of Central Railway Station in 1880 must have been a huge boost to the trade of the pub, which was further advanced by the opening of the Lower Mosley Street Omnibus Station, which opened in 1928.

The bus station was on the corner of Lower Mosley Street and Great Bridgewater Street, and was used by the long distance coach operators offering services to Yorkshire and the Midlands, along with buses from Manchester Corporation and the Stalybridge, Hyde, Mossley and Dukinfield Transport Board. While this created an integrated transport hub, it also provided lots of customers for the Britons Protection so I am not surprised that the pub had a makeover in the 1930s soon after the bus station arrived.

Many of those period features are still in the pub, including the bar and fixed seating, the old bell pushers to summon waiter service and the fireplaces.

The closure of Central Railway Station in 1969 and the bus station in 1973 could have dealt a body blow to the pub, but in

their place have come the Bridgewater Hall and the Exhibition Centre and a growing number of residential properties, which will in turn offer up new customers.

And on the day we called in there was plenty going on. Not that many of the people we encountered had heard of the coach station and only a handful were old enough to have caught a train from what is now G-MEX.

But they all knew the concert hall and the little old lady in tweeds proudly told Peter that she had worked at the Midland Hotel and would occasionally call in at the Briton's Protection with one of "her young men".

I sadly could only admit to one visit and that had been to attend a meeting of which I remember nothing.

Britons Protection 1971

City Road Inn...
the one with lots of names and which looks bigger on the outside.

Now the City Road Inn may date from 1895.

A decade earlier and stretching back almost to the beginning of the 19th century just a few yards away was the the Gaythorn Tavern or Gaythorn Vaults. It was definitely there in 1824 when a Mr. Evan Mawdsley was paying rent to Mr. Thomas Hopwood for the pub which had a rateable value of £35, £13 to £15 above what the immediate neighbours were paying.

And by 1825 this spot was already a prime location surrounded by a mix of industrial properties, which within two decades had expanded to include textile mills, chemical works, a tannery and the gas works, which during the rest of the century just grew and grew.

By 1895 it had been joined by the City Road Inn, which presents a few surprises because it is not

City Road Inn (city Road Hotel) 1970

as big as it looks. The generous will describe it as having two rooms, while others talk of a big room and a darts room.

In its time it has been popular with football fans and those heading off to the clubs, and will have counted plenty of workers from the Gaythorn Gas Works through the door.

It remains at heart a no nonsense, unpretentious place, which is all about meeting friends, drinking beer and having a good time.

But now that Home on First Street has opened for business, showing a mix of interesting films which don't get a showing elsewhere, I think the City Road Inn may get a few more customers.

After all, while there are some interesting restaurants surrounding the cinema, nothing beats a traditional pub as a place to discuss the finer points of the film plot.

And if that plot has been particularly odd or unreal it is all the better that it is talked about in a place which firmly has a foot in reality.

As along as you avoid my friend Eric who has been known to sit outside the pub and tell everyone who is foolish enough to sit near him about his days at the Hacienda.

Eric however fools no one, as his looks and concessionary bus pass are all testimony to that simple fact that he was, even at the height of its popularity, too old to have wandered over the doorstep.

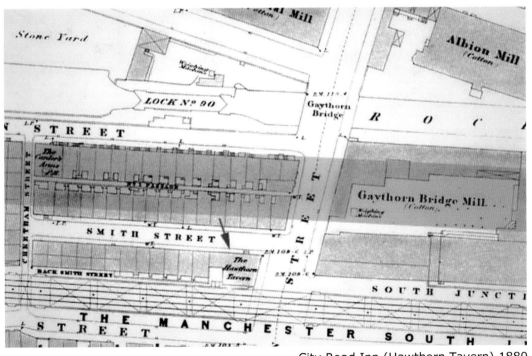

City Road Inn (Hawthorn Tavern) 1880

The Deansgate...

serving beer as the Crown in 1794.

The Deansgate in a way deserves to change its name, it has after all been around since 1794 and may even be older, losing its name only relatively recently when it was briefly Galvins Bar, before becoming the Deansgate.

But while you can change the name of a pub, you can't really take the pub from its name, so any one with a keen eye will see the old name still there in the tiled surround above the first floor windows.

And along with the name there are stories of the place back in the 1960s which Ivy Forth remembered, "didn't do a lot of trade but could be quite busy. On Sunday nights.... I would go down at seven o'clock to open up and the lads would be waiting for me on the doorstep. I knew a lot of the customers; they were people who lived around Deansgate. The lads in the vault were really nice to me. If any of them swore they'd say 'Oi, watch it Ivy's behind the bar!'"*

I doubt that it was ever a quiet place, sandwiched as it was between two sets of railway viaducts, one of which carried trains into Central Station, and the other four lines which ran in to the Great Northern Warehouse.

That said, there is an elegance to the interior. It starts with the wooden panelling and subdued lighting and continues with some pretty nifty seating. I have to say my favourites

The Deansgate (The Crown) 1970

are the carved chairs set back into the wall along with the glass and wooden partitions which also boast some fine carved tracery. Now, not knowing the pub well I have wondered how much of these are original. But even if

they are not the ones polished by Ivy, I like them, and judging by the comments of some of the customers, they do too.

The Deansgate (Crown Hotel) 1940s

The pub is perfectly placed just beyond the metro stop and Deansgate Railway Station to catch a fair amount of "passing trade".

Added to which, I suspect there will be a few from the Beetham Tower who, having experienced 21st century architecture, slide into the Deansgate to be reminded of a more gentle and older style of hospitality.

*The Manchester Village, frank Geaton, 1995, page 30

CASTLEFIELD

A Roman fort, a canal and a museum along with interesting pubs.

Castlefield

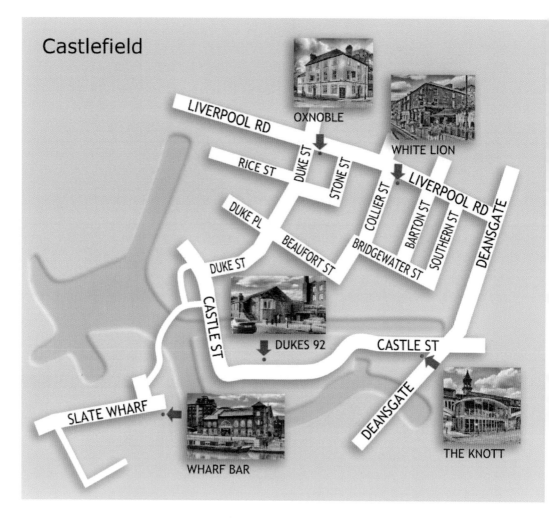

The place that pretty much has cornered the market in our history.... but you won't find a castle at Castlefield.

It is one of those regrettable gaffs that the Normans didn't reckon Manchester important enough for even one of those oddly named Motte and Bailey castles.

However, the disappointed tourist will uncover a rich seam of history which will take them from the Romans to the start of the Age of Canals, and on to the first passenger railway station in the world, some oddly named hospitals and lots of period pubs.

The Romans built a fort here during their push north to subjugate the "blue shield people", who also went under the name of the Brigantes, and were not over keen on hypocausts, Latin or the Roman taxation system.

All of which is why, with minor modification, the fort

continued the business of protecting the important link between Chester and York for 300 years.

In the process, it also attracted a small band of civilians who lived in the township outside its walls, and they have left a mix of everyday objects offering up an insight to how they lived.

As for the fort, bits of its walls survived into the 18th century, which, despite the usual cries from the heritage lobby, were destroyed in the construction of the Duke of Bridgewater's Canal, which, as everyone knows, was constructed to bring coal from the Duke's mines at Worsley into Manchester, thereby providing cheap fuel and further contributing to the grime of the city.

But even before this wanton bit of development, the area had become known as Castlefield, a name which continues to confuse the tourist, especially when confronted with sections of replica Roman wall built in the 1980s by apprentice bricklayers employed by Manchester Corporation.

Sadly, the mural painted by the artist David Vaughan on the side of a nearby railway viaduct showing a group of Roman soldiers entering the fort was left to fade and peel, and was finally painted over.

Still, one of those viaducts was built to resemble the towers of a castle so perhaps all turns out for the best in this best of all possible historical worlds.

From the late 18th century until the 1960s, the area was home to thousands of working families whose everyday existence was bounded by the river to the north, the canals and warehouses to the east and Deansgate to the south.

The warehouses, railway yards and countless small business provided a livelihood for many who lived in the terraced houses off Liverpool Road, and while the churches of St Matthew's and St John's provided for their spiritual needs, there were a range of pubs which offered an alternative haven.

Most have long gone, but there are plenty of stories of the Fox and the Ship which were on Byrom Street, the Victoria on Hardman Street and the Grapes round the corner on Deansgate.*

And some of those stories extend to the few that still straddle Liverpool Road.

*The Manchester Village Compiled by Frank Heaton, 1995

The Oxnoble...

two names and a bit of food history.

The story of the potato which gave its name to the pub is a good one, but didn't stop one of those imaginative souls who hold great sway in the breweries deciding for some odd reason to drop the noble from the title and rename the place the Ox, which may or may not be why there is one of those reproductions of an 18th century print of the said animal above the bar.

Now that in turn is fitting, given that one current pub guide refers to the place as "food led" and while we were there the assistant manager was working hard to accommodate the request of a potential customer for a pre-Christmas birthday meal.

Happily, for me at least the pub has regained its original

Oxnoble 1972

name although what you see today is a much enlarged place. For most of its history it shared the stretch along Liverpool Road up to what is now Stone Street with four other properties.

In the 1930s, Kathleen Ward who lived near the Oxnoble remembered that the main door was on Duke Street, and, "as you went in there was a long lobby and the smoke room was

on the right hand side. Beyond the smoke room were the stairs up to the living accommodation and then the singing room. The lobby went round to the Liverpool Road side and the bar was in the middle.

The vault was at the front and there was a corner door on Liverpool Road where the railway carters used to run in for a drink. There used

to be a long queue of horses and carts on Liverpool Road, especially when the carters were waiting to take their turn on the weighbridge next to City Hall".*

The original deeds of the pub show that the land was sold in 1782 and in 1804 the plot was sold again on condition that it was built on within two years, by which time its rival the White Lion appears to have been up and doing the business of offering beer to its customers for some time.

And for those who want a bit more history, just across the way is the old St Matthews Sunday School built in the 1820s. It has since then gone through many changes, but has always been a popular choice for those who wanted a set of offices or studios which had just that bit more of a presence.

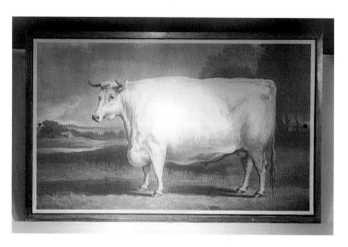

It belonged to St Matthew's Church which was a little further up Liverpool Road on the other side. Sadly, it went a long time ago, as did the properties which fronted Tonman Street.

It was during the demolition of these that a bit of our Roman past was revealed, and like others I wandered down to the site. In my case it was with a party of Year 7s out from Wythenshawe on the 100 bus.

And now there is a lasting monument to those Romans in the form of the reconstructed walls of the old fort which were built by apprentices from the Direct Works division of Manchester Corporation.

Sacks of potatoes from Potato Wharf 1924

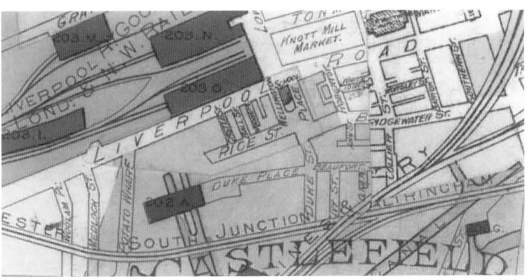

Liverpool Road circa 1880s

* ibid The Manchester Village page 29

The White Lion...

offering beer and cheer for centuries.

There will be many who have their own stories to tell of nights in the White Lion. Mine only go back to the 1980s, but two decades before that the place was run by Gerry and Sophia Ennis who described how they built the business up from three and half barrels a week to fourteen, which was all the more impressive given that pubs closed in the afternoons and called time at 10.30 during week nights.

Mr. Ennis was happy to close at 2.00pm on a Sunday and see his customers move down to the Oxnoble "which was a great gambling house, and they'd stay there all afternoon".*

More recently, the White Lion has added a beer garden bordering the heritage park, where those with a powerful imagination can think themselves back to when the original Roman fort stood not far away.

For those with children, I suspect that, after the beer, soft drinks and assorted pub food, it will be a game of chase the kids into the ditches which front the fort.

White Lion 1972

A pastime which might have been indulged in by unhappy Britons who, having slid into the original ditches with a plan to scale the walls of the fort, found themselves trapped by the cunning Roman design of making the sides vertical and hence impossible to climb out of.

On a lighter note, those preferring the inside of the White Lion can spend their time looking at the Manchester United

memorabilia or the pictures of member of the cast of Coronation Street, some of whom regularly made their way across from Granada Studios.

I can't be sure, but that walk would most likely have taken them along Lower Byrom Street up Tonman Street and beside what had once been the grounds of St. Matthew's Church.

Easy enough today, but fraught with dangers in the 1850s, when one report commented on how the authorities had been forced to put planking up above the church wall to prevent piles of rubbish dumped in Tonman Street from invading the grounds.

* ibid The Manchester Village page 29

The Knott...
underneath the arches.

If you are old enough to remember Flanagan and Alan singing "Underneath the Arches", then putting a bar inside a viaduct has got to be an improvement on sheltering from the rain.

And Castlefield has more than its fair share of viaducts. Once the viaducts criss-crossed the area carrying goods into Liverpool Road and the Great Northern Warehouse, as well as passengers on their way to Central Railway Station and where there are viaducts there are arches, and arches mean businesses, from lock up garages to workshops and much more.

The Knott (The Modern Tyre Repair Co Ltd) 1966

After all, the arch is a perfect space which otherwise would go to waste, and the railway companies were quick to see the potential, renting them out and using them also for stables for their huge number of horses.

So just down on Water Street back in the late 1980s, I

stumbled across the remains of one set of stables still with their wooden pens.

We tend to forget just how much was shifted by horse and cart in the past. Each railway

company had their own stables and in all there were 157 carriers listed in the 1911 street directory.

In a trip round London Road in the 1970s, my old friend Norman remembered an event forty years earlier, when a horse pulling a full load lost its footing on Stony Brew, which is the steep incline leading from Ducie Street to Store Street. The carter couldn't regain control and the horse, wagon and driver crashed into a wall at the bottom.

None of which has anything to do with the Knott Bar, save that it occupies an arch and that once, not that long ago the same space was filled with the sound of a motor mechanic at work. Nor was this motor mechanic the only one in the area. Garages along with printing firms were fairly common right up to recent times, with the last printing company on the corner of Southern Street shutting down, about the same time that Andrew's Garages also on Southern Street closed.

And for those who preferred buying new and exciting vehicles, there was that motor bike shop on the corner of Liverpool Road and Southern Street. It outlasted most of the other "shops" but it too has gone.

All of which brings me back to the Knott which is a pleasant place to while away the time in an arch.

The bar is light and modern in appearance, but the brickwork and the stone arch remind you exactly where you are, which may inspire a visit to Knott Mill Station directly opposite, which in turn offers the pub quiz buff a host of possible subjects starting with its name.

It may now be called Deansgate, but it retains its original name high up on the building, while just a short walk away is the site of the emergency hospital established after the outbreak of cholera in 1832.

Dr Gautier, who wrote a book on the epidemic, records that some of the first 200 cases of cholera occurred in Castlefield, and fifteen years later three people caught the disease in Southern Street, one on Liverpool Road and three on Camp Street.

But enough of such grim tales. To lighten the mood, there is always the short walk on the last leg of the Rochdale Canal, which can be accessed from directly opposite the Knott Bar, and by degrees takes you to Dukes 92 and The Wharf.

Dukes 92...
a much visited pub and restaurant.

Anyone who takes the trip along the stretch of the Rochdale Canal from the Dale Street Basin in Piccadilly to Castlefield will be rewarded with some fine things to see. These include the old power station, which, along with generating electricity, provided steam to heat the nearby offices through huge pipes which leaked in places, causing more than a bit of concern to the nervous.

For those in the know, the canal runs under office blocks, past the old St Mary's hospital and down toward Dukes 92. Once (and not that long ago) there were two half submerged boats belonging to the old Rochdale Canal Company, just past the Deansgate bridge, but they are gone and the curious tourist must be content with the restored lock keeper's house,

Dukes 92 (Lock 92) 1960

and the final set of lock gates marking the end of the canal's passage into Castlefield.

But the attractions of Dukes 92 compensate for the absence of sunken boats. It was opened in 1991, just as the regeneration of the area was underway and takes its name from those last set of gates which are number 92.

Along with a spacious inside with exposed brick work and wooden beams, the pub has that waterside spot, which allows you to sit on a fine day with a glass and some food and wait for a passing boat to navigate the lock.

Some years ago, I got the chance to travel the stretch up to Piccadilly, which was fun, if hard work, given the number of locks, and which back then had to be completed to a strict timetable. Since then, I have tended to watch others navigate their way along the water way.

And it has to be said that, for some at least, the knowledge that by the time they have passed Dukes 92, navigation becomes more pleasant as, by then, there is just that last lock and the basin where they can berth the boat.

Perhaps unfairly, the leg through east Manchester has gained a bad reputation for some unpleasant experiences, while I am not alone in encountering the odd floating thing at Piccadilly.

At the entrance to Lock 92 1972

And it was back there that my old friend Norman, who had been born around 1910 in St Andrews Street, was taught to swim by that simple practice of being thrown into the canal by his dad.

Sitting watching from the bar is, I am sure you will agree, a much better option.

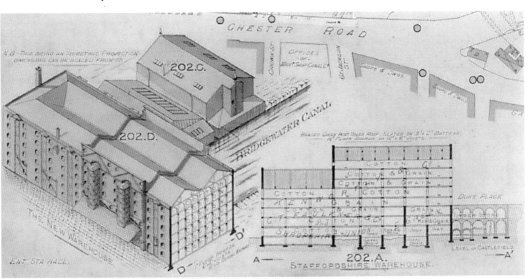

Warehouses alongside Bridgewater Canal 1820s

The Wharf...
the pub that looks the part.

Now for anyone who wandered around the Castlefield canal basin long before it became fashionable, the Wharf presents a problem. I know I was one of them and spent part of a day trying to work out the origins of the building.

For some it does not look out of place seeming to blend with the warehouses nearby and yet, while those warehouses date back into the early 19th century, it was only built in 1998. Added to which, the Wharf which now occupies the building opened in 2012.

That said, it is an interesting place extending over three floors, although the uppermost level consists of what our hosts

354

Potato Wharf 1961

admitted was just a small gallery reserved for those wanting a private and intimate space for a romantic evening.

The rest is open plan, tastefully laid out with big windows, affording fine views of the Merchants Warehouse and the Middle Warehouse, which were constructed in the late 1820s.

And if you tire of looking at them, there are always the boats moored alongside, which are as colourful as they are varied in their design.

Now of course the best time to be in the canal basin at the Wharf is on a warm sunny day when the attractions of the pub's garden are all too obvious, but on a day when the rain is coming down like stair rods and there is a viciously cold wind cutting across the open water, then the interior of the pub has a lot to offer, including the upside down picture.

The purists may be a tad put out that this is not from Manchester, but advertises a show put on at the Theatre Royal Covent Garden in the spring of 1826, but for those with time to spare and a desire to impress their friends there is a challenge here to correctly read the listed events.

Nor should we be over sniffy at the choice of poster; there are plenty of older and traditional pubs across the city which in

the past have shown off paintings of long dead foreign monarchs, more than a few views of the Highland glens and collections of faded picture postcards from places as exotic as Cleethorpes, the Costa del Sol and Margate, all sent from long forgotten customers.

And no doubt, when I am next in the Wharf, there will be pinned behind the bar a picture post card from Ron and Tina showing a canal berth somewhere in the Midlands with the message of, "how much we enjoyed our time in the pub while moored along the towpath".

ALL SAINTS

Just over the road on Cavendish Street was the old Town Hall.

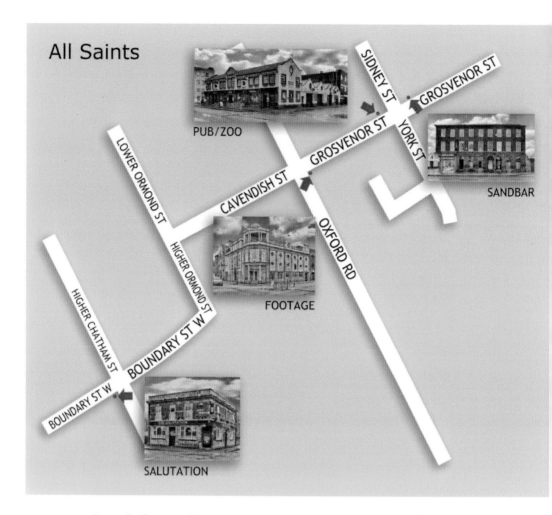

PUB/ZOO

SANDBAR

FOOTAGE

SALUTATION

South from the bend in the river Medlock along the Oxford Road corridor.... bright new universities an old church and a reminder that this was once not Manchester.

The stretch of Oxford Road from the river down towards the twin universities means many things to many people. For some it is just the bus that takes you to Rusholme, Withington and Didsbury.

For generations of students it was the route that dropped them off at the University, John Dalton College and the School of Art.

Nor could anyone mistake the University because some bus conductors would announce that we had arrived at "debtors haven", "lazybone palace" and "dossers playground".

And for many others this was still a strip with plenty of

shops, more than a few offices, workshops and a cinema.

Back in the early 1970s, the one that caught my eye and continues to intrigue me was "Carroll Arden .... Stylist to the Stars". The shop which harked back to an earlier time stood just a short distance from "On the Eighth Day" which offered up an alternative life style of joss sticks, homemade organic perfume and stacks of jewellery with stylish clothes including rails of loons.*

And just over the road on Cavendish Street was the old Town Hall which is a reminder that we are in Chorlton-upon-Medlock, a place which had its own governance and didn't become part of Manchester until 1838. The Town Hall may have been a more modest affair than its rival in the heart of the city, but for seven years it oversaw the running of the area.

I am not sure it fared so well after 1838, but it served the community as a venue for all sorts of activities including the location for the Fifth Pan African Congress in 1945, famous because here gathered together were many who would lead their countries after independence.

And I remember attending a series of events in there, and liked the entrance with its modest but elegant staircase that led up to the public hall, but by the late 1960s it was looking its age and in 1970 the interior was removed, a new one substituted and it became part of Manchester Polytechnic.

Next door is the School of Art which was completed in 1881, while almost opposite and completed in the same year is the Ormond Building which was home to the Poor Law Guardians who administered the Chorlton Union.

Town Hall Chorlton-on-Medlock 1833

*Loon pants were the fashion statement in the 1970s with their huge bell bottom style.

Sandbar...

once two elegant town houses and later became a factory and warehouse.

The Sandbar is the one which looks to inhabit what might have been elegant homes of the middling people, and, sure enough, back in 1850 one was home to a merchant, and the other a surgeon.

But these were no palaces set in a leafy suburb. Hard by the houses were timber and stone yards and a maze of terraced housing and as early as the 1860s our two properties were given over to a series of different commercial and industrial uses from a fancy box maker, to an upholsterer, a corn merchant and in the 1970s a warehouse. All of which I suppose

Sandbar 1963

offers up that tantalizing thought that could the walls talk, what a set of tales they would tell.

And no less interesting, but perhaps over a shorter time span might be the stories from Pub/Zoo which is also on Grosvenor Street.

And those from the surrounding area which has developed apace with blocks of student accommodation stretching back

from All Saints towards Hulme, the relocation of the old Didsbury College of Education into a modern building at Birley, and the expansion of the Victoria University sitting beside the ever expanding MMU.

That amazing transformation is also reflected in the strip of shops opposite

All Saints for where once "Carroll Arden cut, dried and "permed" the row is pretty much fast food outlets serving the needs of students on the move between lectures.

Even the 1940's Post Office now offers a range of quick things to eat while watching the buses pass in a seemingly endless stream.

And for anyone wanting further confirmation of the all-pervading presence of students and their teachers, some would argue all you have to do is linger in the four pubs on the walk.

Sandbar (Ridgeway Stores) 1973

Pub/Zoo...

two pubs for the price of one.

Now, according to a good friend, Pub/Zoo was launched onto the scene twenty or so years ago as an Irish pub and I remember passing it when it was called "The Pub".

But long before that, it was home to several businesses including Duncan and Foster, Roland and Rifkin, "high class fashion workshop" and in 1969 A.B. Barber & Co,

"manufactures of children's wear".

All of that said, for what was once a humble workshop, the more I look at it the more it grows on me, although it cannot compare with the old Grosvenor cinema on the opposite side of the road. Or for that matter some of the grand new buildings

which are part of the "university quarter" just a few yards up the road.

As early as 1945, the City of Manchester's plan for the future had designated Grosvenor Square as the campus for the city's colleges and this was confirmed in 1972 when the Polytechnic announced that this would be the hub for many of its operations, leading to the demolition of the surrounding buildings and retaining only the School of Art and the Town Hall.

It was a grand plan which led some students to ponder in a

Pub/Zoo (Duncan & Fosters) 1973

All Saints 1849

conspiratorial way that this would effectively lump almost all the student population in one small area thereby making it easier for the authorities to respond to the sort of student upheaval which had been part of the late 1960s and early 70s.

Footage...

cream and green with a cinematic story.

The Grosvenor was opened in 1915 to a design by Percy Hothersall and with almost a thousand seats was, I think, the biggest cinema outside the city centre at the time. Even now, long after its days as a place to see films have ceased, it is still a pretty impressive building.

Its green and cream terra cotta tiles marked it out on that stretch of Oxford Road, which apart from the Town Hall opposite and the old offices of the Poor Law Union on the corner of Cavendish Street, was a drab spot.

And I just missed going there. It closed as a cinema in 1968 and I had to be content with using it as a pub, which it had become after unsuccessful stints as a bingo hall and snooker venue.

Some of the original features still exist including the balcony, vaulted ceiling and much plaster work, although they have not been treated well.

Footage (Grosvenor) 1935

But on a Saturday night I must say that the upper level has something going for it which has much to do with those porthole windows with their coloured glass.

I guess the cinema entrepreneur, H.D. Moorhouse would be less than amused. Pretty much all his working life was given over to picture houses and films; having started as an

accountant, he got drawn in with a part share on one and later a string of cinemas, across the city.

He may, however, have approved the changes made to the old Till & Kennedy Building which stands next to the Art School

on Cavendish Street and is well worth a look.

It was built in 1905 for William Righton whose name appears above the main entrance. He was a draper and the

building offers up plenty of clues to its origins as a drapers shop.

The spacious ground floor was perfect for accommodating a vast range of fabrics, while the large windows allowed the maximum amount of daylight into the building, a feature complemented by the top-lit gallery with the cutaway floor, providing extra light to penetrate down into the main shop.

Now this had always puzzled me, as had the benching around the gallery, and only now have I discovered that these benches were where "the cloth was measured".

The Salutation...

serving beer from 1825 with a claim on Charlotte Bronte and saved by a university.

I came very late to the Salutation. In fact, despite knowing about it for a full four decades, I went there for the first time just five years ago.

I was in the company of my old friend Joe, and having done an exhibition at the Art College, we fell into the pub and spent an enjoyable afternoon. Unlike me, it has been one of Joe's haunts from when he was a student at the College and its mix of good beer, interesting characters and historic setting regularly drew him back, but I have to confess I knew nothing of its history until I read that the Manchester Metropolitan University gave a substantial amount of money to restore the place back in 2014.*

And I am glad they did, given that the pub has real history.

Salutation Hotel 1959

Elizabeth Beverley was running the pub from 1833, and, before that, the landlord was Thomas Beverley. Thomas remains a shadowy figure who appears in the rate records living in different parts of the city and may have had various jobs before becoming a publican, but, as yet, it is unclear whether he was here when the pub first opened its doors sometime around 1825.

And I wonder if he would have approved of the blue plaque on the side of the building which records that in 1846, "The Revd. Patrick Bronte came to Manchester for a cataract operation accompanied by his daughter Charlotte. They took lodgings at 59 Boundary Street West (formerly known as 83 Mount Pleasant).

"It was here that Charlotte began to write her first successful novel, Jane Eyre".

Now, given that it is on the side of the wall, the curious and the interested might well draw a conclusion about the pub and the Bronte family, but their lodgings were not here. Still, it remains a nice thought.

And if the Bronte family were able, after the passage of 170 years or so, to visit the pub, they might approve of the decor. It is warm, has a period looking fireplace and mirror and more than a few tiled areas, none of which may exactly be contemporary with Miss Bronte, but may be far more comfortable than the lodgings they took close by.

Of course we will never know, but after the third pint I don't suppose most of us would care.

*Joy as 170-year-old Hulme pub gets £235k makeover, March 2014

Epilogue by CAMRA

"Manchester has everything but a beach" said Stones Roses front man Ian Brown. The city certainly overflows with great beer and breweries – both are celebrated by locals and visitors, and it's a rare week there's not something to delight the drinker.

Pub history is beautifully illustrated in this book, but the explosion of events over the past five years seems destined for a worthy sequel. The traditional family brewers who survived consumer and planning changes at the turn of the century have been joined by smaller and more experimental brewers who flourish as the trade tie weakened. Brewery tap events have opened up areas of the city previously deserted most weekends. The Greater Manchester area has over 80 breweries, and Manchester and Stockport boast eponymous Beer Weeks to attract both casual and dedicated drinkers.

Over the years we have seen some dramatic changes in the City's layout and composition especially relating to its pub heritage. With several of our favourite and historic pubs being demolished (Tommy Ducks) closed (The Old Grapes) and threatened with closure (Sir Ralph Abercromby) Manchester City has managed to retain many of its gems, many of which feature in this book. Additionally many new and outstanding new bars have been created (Port Street Beer House, Pie & Ale, Allotment, Soup Kitchen, Cafe Beermoth, Brink, Gaslamp, Gasworks Brewbar, Pilcrow) and the future looks bright. Maybe in 50 years they will feature in a book similar to this? Who knows?

The city centre now has its own CAMRA branch, allowing the other seven Greater Manchester branches to focus on campaigning across the region. But all come together to present the largest beer and cider festival in the North each January, timed just as the naysayers and abstinence merchants are wringing their hands. Typical of Manchester. Now, where are the buckets and spades?

Central Manchester branch, CAMRA

Manchester and the Great War

A new book by Andrew Simpson which draws on a vast collection of material never before seen. Including letters, official documents, photographs, and a wealth of everyday objects, which include picture postcards, souvenirs and very personal family memorials dedicated to all those who died in action.

Available in all good book stores.

Paintings from Pictures

All the paintings that appear in this book are available to buy either on 7mm white painted MDF board with a brush stroke varnish finish or as an A3 giclee print.

For further information get in touch with Peter by email at peter@paintingsfrompictures.co.uk or Telephone 07521 557888

Other Books by The Authors

Local artist Peter Topping and historian Andrew Simpson are working together on a series of collaborations including paintings and stories about Chorlton and Manchester. For more information contact us at www.gladtobe.in or contact Peter on 07521 557888.